TRUCK NUTS

THE FAST LANE TRUCK's GUIDE TO PICKUPS

Kent "Mr. Truck" Sundling
Andre Smirnov

For permission requests, please contact the publisher at:

Mango Publishing Group
2850 S. Douglas Road, 3rd Floor
Coral Gables, FL 33134 USA
info@mango.bz

For special orders, quantity sales, course adoptions and corporate sales, please email the publisher at sales@mango.bz. For trade and wholesale sales, please contact Ingram Publisher Services at customer.service@ingramcontent.com or +1.800.509.4887.

TRUCK NUTS:
The Fast Lane Truck's Guide to Pickups
Reprint Edition 2017

Library of Congress Cataloging

Names: Sundling, Kent and Smirnov, Andre
Title: Truck Nuts / by Kent Sundling and Andre Smirnov
Library of Congress Control Number: 2017934258
ISBN 9781633534858 (paperback), ISBN 9781633534865(eBook) BISAC Category Code: TRA001150 TRANSPORTATION/ Automotive/Trucks

ISBN: (hardcover or paperback) 978-1-63353-485-8,
(ebook) 978-1-63353-486-5

Printed in the United States of America

DEDICATION

From Kent:

Dedicated to my mother who I lost to cancer when I was five years old. She died four months before her first grandchild was born. This is why you'll see my grandchildren in many of my truck review videos. I cherish all the time I can spend with them; they like new trucks, too.

From Andre:

Thank you to my beautiful wife Samantha and my family for supporting my dream.

And to all of the great Truck Nuts who read TFLtruck.com news and watch TFLtruck videos every day: thank you all for your support and for making this book possible!

CONTENTS

ROMAN MICA

FOREWORD

Roman Mica
Founder of TFLTruck

I dare you to Google "Truck Nuts". The results you get back might be considered by some NSFW (Not Safe For Work), so consider yourself warned.

When it comes to this book's authors, Kent Sundling (Mr. Truck) and Andre Smirnov, both of these longtime automotive journalists are truly nuts about trucks.

Instead of blood, diesel runs through their arteries and veins. They tow in their sleep, roll coal for breakfast, go wheelin' for lunch, and blast up the Ike Gauntlet with 24,000 pounds of WWII White M3 Half Track for dinner. If you need to Google any of these terms, chances are you're reading the wrong book.

But if you love all things trucks (and that includes hauling, off-roading, towing, wheeling, drag racing, and most importantly torque and horsepower), you've come to the right place.

Truck Nuts is not just a guide to the modern pickup truck, but most importantly a love letter to the most important tool in any working man's or woman's tool box....the all-American pickup truck.

Unlike most cars, modern trucks are used for so much more than just getting from point A to point B. They are a hunter's best friend, a working man or woman's most capable tool, and a truck enthusiast's most important possession. In short, today's pickup truck embodies the pioneer spirit rendered in iron, aluminum, and leather; the spirit that built America from sea to shining sea.

Sit back and relax and let Mr. Truck and Andre be your guide to all things truck. If you love Chevy, Ford, or Ram, if you are a longtime Toyota or Nissan guy or gal, or if you simply want to jump into the truck pool...***Truck Nuts*** is the book for you.

Jump in, the water's warm, the trucks are all here. Let Mr. Truck and Andre enlighten, inform, and entertain you, so that by Chapter 16 you won't have to Google Ike Gauntlet, but instead you'll be part of the TFL's truck tribe.

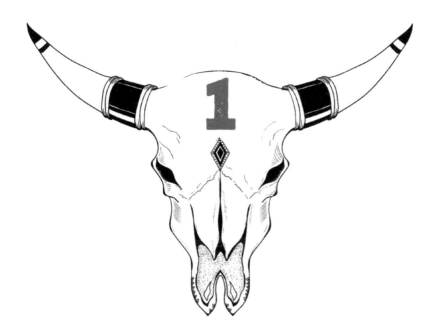

AMERICA'S LOVE AFFAIR

WITH THE

PICKUP TRUCK

WHY TRUCKS?

MR. TRUCK

Where do large pickup trucks roam free? America! The only place in the world where you can find pickup trucks around every corner. America is in love with trucks, and the affair is stronger than ever. We are conceived in trucks, born in trucks, live in trucks, work in trucks, have fun in trucks, and die in trucks. Is there any other way?

Mr. Truck with a B.S. in Trucknology,
my office has 4 wheels and a view of the Rockies.

Who would choose a car over a truck? Trucks give you a feeling of power and safety. You are the king of the road in a truck. Cars are vehicles you lay down in and crawl out of. Trucks are like sitting at your kitchen table, easy to climb into and slide out of. Trucks can offer benefits for your dating game.

Get close and cuddle up on a bench seat without a console getting stuck up your differential. Who needs a backseat! You can't even reach the A/C from there. Have you ever seen a car with a rifle rack? Doubtful. You get to see a lot more scenery from your truck.

You know truckers have an advantage looking down into convertibles.

Trucks are as American as baseball, hot dogs, and apple pie. Everywhere you turn, pickups are there. They are lined up at the local bar like the horses were tied up outside an old West saloon. When you arrive at the church, some of those same trucks are there as well.

There is a variety of trucks, from minis to midsize, from half-tons to heavy duties, and beyond. There are also as many unique and customized trucks as there are truck owners.

If you have the money, you can accessorize your truck with all the fancy toys cars come with. I am talking about the giant sunroof, massaging and cooled seats, heated steering wheel, and a fully-integrated smartphone interface.

You can go above and beyond with decorating your truck: huge mud flaps, headache rack, semi-style exhaust stacks, hood ornaments, bull bumper, running boards, and stickers.

When you own a truck, everyone wants to borrow it. Why not, can you haul horses, cows, compost, lawn mowers, firewood, or giant furniture in a car?

The pickup I learned to drive first was Dad's 1953 Ford three-quarter ton. I learned to do those famous "Jack Rabbit starts" as dad would call them when I was twelve years old. I enjoyed immensely when my boys started to drive. They would help me fix fence with the dually. It took both of them to push in the clutch to start it. I would wave to them from down the fence line to bring up the truck, and I would see their little heads bobbing up and down above the steering wheel as they struggled to push in the clutch.

BRAGGING RIGHTS

Competition Created
the American Free Enterprise System

For three out of the ten years I sold trucks, I was an auto broker. Most of the time I was working for AAA Auto Club, buying vehicles for the membership; I've sold all the major makes and models. Most people become loyal to one brand. But it's good to compare. Competition is what improves things. The Japanese taught us valuable lessons in the 80s on how to build cars. We as humans are such emotional buyers. We seldom do what's best for us. And of course marketing rules the earth. That's why the best diet in the world is shutting off the TV during commercials! Back to trucks, competition helps us in so many ways. The top brands usually alternate leadership with each new model. There is a difference in areas like diesels and transmissions.

"The Right Truck"

I learned how to buy the right truck by, you guessed it, by buying the wrong one a few times! Since my first trucks were used, I had no idea of what the manufacturer's gross vehicle weight rating or warranty requirements were all about. I hauled 3,000 pounds in my half-ton, 5,000 pounds in my three-quarter ton, and 10,000 pounds in my tonner. Oops, that was probably a little too much. That could explain why so many u-joints, clutches and brakes had to be replaced.

It's hard to recommend which truck without knowing what you are going to use it for. Half tons are generally used for the light work, loaded occasionally. Three-quarter tons and one-tons can be loaded all the time just like their cousins, the 18-wheeler. The heavy-duty three-quarter and 1 tons used to only ride nice when they were loaded. They have come a long way, baby. Now they all ride like cars. In the big cities, people use them as cars. When I first came to Denver, I was amazed to see five-year-old pickups with no scratches in the beds. My pickups didn't last the first day without a scratch. After you drop the first salt block and the first big round bale, the bed just doesn't look the same.

Our affair with the pickup truck will continue as long as the old glory continues to wave. Is there any other way to explain it?

ANDRE SMIRNOV

Perhaps, there is another way to look at why we are nuts about trucks.

What is the most popular vehicle in America? Is it a family sedan or a crossover? Nope! It is the Ford F-Series truck, and it has been this way for nearly four decades, or this is what Ford will have you believe. General Motors outsold Ford trucks a few times, but who's counting? In fact, we at TFLtruck.com and MrTruck.com are the ones counting and monitoring every breath of the pickup truck industry, as do all the manufacturers.

The main point remains the same: pickup trucks rule the sales charts in the United States. Don't believe us? Take a quick look at the numbers! Combined, there were 1,278,941 pickup trucks sold in the United States during the first half of 2016, and nearly all makes showed positive growth. In comparison, 1,111,344 mid-size sedans were purchased over the same period, while showing an overall downward trend. There may be just one other automotive market segment with sales numbers that challenge trucks: the compact crossover segment. These lifted AWD wagon-looking things are the craze in recent years.

A LITTLE ABOUT ME

I immigrated to the United States from Russia in 1992 and came straight to Colorado. This is the land of opportunity and freedom. There are very few countries in the world where any person can go from nothing to a self-made success story. The United States is the best environment for promoting innovation and the entrepreneurial spirit. All it takes for success is hard work.

My American Dream is here and it's still evolving, and pickup trucks are at the center of it all. I began towing trailers and truckin' as a regular consumer in the early 2000s. Now, trucks are my life, and what a great life it is!

Andre Smirnov and Mr. Truck (Kent Sundling)

So why do pickup trucks kick ass? Why are they so popular? Why are we so crazy nuts about them? Here are the top five reasons why trucks rule!

5.
Tax Benefits

This is perhaps the least understood of all the reasons. It applies to vehicles that are used for business purposes. Vehicles with Gross Vehicle Weight Rating (GVWR) of more than 6,000 pounds and less than 14,000 pounds are eligible for the largest tax deduction in accordance with Section 179 (Note: details available here: http://www.section179.org/section_179_vehicle_deductions.html).

There is a requirement that the miles driven in the vehicle for business purposes constitute at least 50 percent of all miles. Commuting to work does not qualify as business use. Guess what? All Class 1 (half-ton), Class 2 (three-quarter ton), and Class 3 (one-ton) pickup trucks are within this weight range and qualify for a tax deduction. Cargo vans and some shuttle/passenger vans also qualify for this. This can even be attributed to used trucks, but at a lesser deduction. Unfortunately, midsize pickup trucks such as the Toyota Tacoma and the Chevrolet Colorado do not qualify for the maximum deduction.

Please consult with your tax attorney or CPA for specific details on how this may apply to your case.

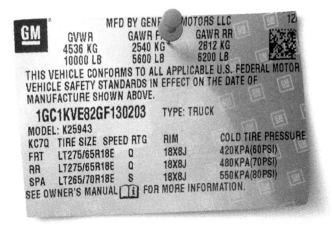

GVWR is the maximum weight your truck is rated to carry (without a trailer in tow). This is the empty curb weight of your truck plus all the people and cargo in it. The GVWR rating for your specific truck can be found on a card that is mounted inside the driver's door jam.

4.
Off-Road Capability

Pickup trucks may not be the ultimate off-road vehicles in the world. This title goes to the body-on-frame SUVs such as the Mercedes-Benz G-wagon, Jeep Wrangler, and Land Rover Defender. However, pickup trucks are no slouches when it comes time to leave pavement and explore the world.

These trucks are adorned with well-known and respected off-road designations: Nissan PRO-4X, Toyota TRD Pro, Ram Rebel, Ram Power Wagon, GMC All Terrain, Chevrolet Z71, Ford FX4, and the Ford Raptor.

All pickups can be equipped with specific off-road hardware for tackling serious terrain. This includes underbody skid plates, differential lockers, two-speed 4x4 transfer cases, ample ground clearance, off-road biased tires, and sophisticated terrain management systems that adjust traction control, antilock brakes, and other systems for optimal off-road performance.

In fact, the 2016 Ram Power Wagon is equipped with electrically locking front and rear axles, a disconnectable front sway bar that allows for greater axle articulation, skid plates, beefy Goodyear Wrangler tires, and a factory-installed winch up front. No wonder it won TFLtruck's 2016 Gold Hitch: Best Off-Road Truck Award. More on this in a later Chapter.

3.
Manufacturer Rebates

The automotive world is highly competitive, but the pickup truck segment is even more so due to closely matched products and an overwhelming variety of options. Pickup trucks have a large profit margin baked in from the start. Truck manufacturers often dip into the profit margin with sizable rebates on new trucks in order to gain a competitive advantage. The consumer is the winner. Enough said.

2.
Great Value

You get a lot more metal for your hard-earned dollar. A truck can perform many functions. It's a Swiss Army knife in your toolbox of life. You could be a one vehicle household if you owned a pickup, but it will be difficult to complete all your projects and activities if you only own a sedan. You can enjoy the benefits of an open bed to carry bulky items, a large cab to carry your favorite people, a robust 4-wheel drive system for rough weather or off-road adventures, and a towing capacity to move some heavy trailers. You get an awful lot for your money with a truck.

1.
'Merica

How do you define the American Dream? It is a land of opportunity and freedom. All you have to do is go out there and grab your piece of the dream. Take it by the horns, wrestle it down, and reap the rewards of your hard work. And what better way to do it than in a pickup truck?

Most small, medium, and large businesses own pickup trucks in their fleets. Most contractors and do-it-yourselfers use pickups to get the job done. If there is an opportunity out there, the pickup will help you seize it. Trucks don't have to be used for work.

Those who work hard play even harder. The pickup is once again there to assist. Whether it's getting out of a neighborhood after a major snow storm to go skiing, helping a friend move, traveling to a remote location for a weekend of camping, towing a fishing boat to the lake, or having a fun tailgate party, a pickup truck is your friend.

Trucks will even handle extreme or unusual circumstances: delivering supplies to a flood-stricken area, helping take people to safety after a natural disaster or a man-made crisis. Pickups are very proficient at carrying people and/or cargo, and trucks are getting ever better at their task.

M923 Military 6x6 5-ton Truck

Crew cab trucks are the most popular kind of pickups sold. They serve as a family hauler and a job-site worker all in one. They offer the ability to transport five people (six people in some cases), and there is a truck bed behind to carry any cargo or whatever junk you choose.

Mr. Truck: Whoa Andre! Easy there! It's much simpler than that. Truck owners don't take orders. We are our own bosses! If our trucks cannot do something today, we will modify them to get the job done tomorrow. It is the essence of the independent and free American spirit. You cannot put numbers on this!

Andre: Sure you can put numbers on it, Kent. No other vehicle on the market offers as many variations or configurations as trucks do. There are literally millions of ways you can configure your truck from the factory. There are three cab sizes, three bed length options, many engine choices, 2WD or 4x4, trim levels, colors, appearance packages, and optional equipment. It is the freedom of choice, and your ability to select a unique configuration for your next truck that nobody else has. You will not see yourself coming and going at the next traffic light if you are in a pickup.

Ram Trucks offer thirty-one custom colors for their heavy-duty trucks. If you want your Ram HD to be painted School Bus Yellow, all you have to do is pay a little extra. As long as they have more than ten orders for a Ram Power Wagon of a custom color, they will make it so.

Did you know that ever more manufacturers are coming to the American market with pickup truck offerings? The "big five" are already here: Ford, GM, Nissan, Ram, and Toyota. That's right. The big five, not the big three. Nissan is coming back in a big way with the all-new Nissan Titan truck lineup. Toyota just completely redesigned the Tacoma.

Now, Honda is bringing back the Ridgeline, and there are rumors of the next generation Ford Ranger, Jeep Wrangler pickup, Hyundai Santa Cruz, and Ram midsize pickup truck going on sale before the end of this decade. It's never been a better time for pickup trucks.

Where Do Trucks Go From Here?

Expect to see pickups evolve along with the passenger car. The following areas of development that will be hotly contested over the next decade are: diesel, hybrid and electric powertrains, usage of advanced lightweight materials such as carbon fiber or Barotex, and autonomous driving.

Government Corporate Average Fuel Economy (CAFE) standards are getting more and more stringent. Large, light truck EPA combined economy averages for the fleet stay at 19 MPG until 2021, but then sharply grow to 23 MPG by 2025. Basically, all trucks sold in a given year by a manufacturer must meet these efficiency goals after you average all of them out. Failure to do so will result in penalties.

Many companies are already working on turbo-diesel, hybrid, plug-in hybrid, or electric trucks to satisfy tougher efficiency standards. The push for higher efficiency must examine lightweight building materials. Performance and luxury cars rely on carbon fiber to reduce weight and improve performance.

Why can't a pickup truck be made out of carbon fiber? There is also a new type of fiber, called Barotex (http://www.barotex.com). Proliferation of driver-aid technologies will culminate in a pickup truck that operates autonomously. It's a matter of when, not if. More on this in another Chapter.

Let the pickup truck love affair continue!

Being an automotive journalist in Colorado has its perks. This was in Estes Park, where the elk run free. This is a redneck paradise for Mr. Truck.

ANDRE

2

TORTURING TRUCKS IS A GOOD THING

INTRODUCTION TO TFLTRUCK TESTING

IKE GAUNTLET: EXTREME TOWING TEST

You know Dwight D. Eisenhower as a five-star US Army General during World War II, as the Supreme Commander of the Allied Forces in Europe, and as the 34th President of the United States.

As history would have it, then US Army Major, D. Eisenhower was assigned to a transcontinental military convoy in 1919 with a goal of testing vehicles—trucks—and drumming up support for road improvements across the country. Indeed, the convoy averaged five miles per hour from Washington D.C. to San Francisco, California. Eisenhower's efforts, war and military experience, and the tension of the Cold War with the Soviet Union culminated in President Eisenhower signing the Interstate Highway System project into law via the Federal Aid Highway Act. The goals of the project were to improve efficiency of military operations, to speed up potential city evacuation procedures, and to stimulate economic growth. The rest is history. The project was and still is essential to making our daily lives easier.

Today, you can complete the transcontinental Washington D.C. to San Francisco 2,812 mile journey in about forty-two hours if you drive at an average 67 miles per hour.

Eisenhower/Johnson Memorial Tunnels

Why digress into Dwight Eisenhower's history? It has everything to do with extreme towing tests in our home state of Colorado. The two-lane westbound Eisenhower Tunnel was completed in 1973. It was later joined by the east-bound Edwin C. Johnson Tunnel that was finished in 1979. Edwin Johnson was a Colorado governor and US Senator who lobbied for the Interstate System to be built across Colorado. The Eisenhower/Johnson Memorial Tunnels are the longest mountain tunnels in the country, and represent the highest elevation for the entire US Interstate Highway System. The highest elevation of the tunnels at the western portal is at 11,158 feet above sea level, and the slightly longer eastbound tunnel stretches for 1.697 miles. The tunnels also cut through the Continental Divide in the Rocky Mountains.

How do you get to the western portal for these tunnels? It's a grueling eight mile climb on Interstate 70 from Dillon, Colorado, and all the way to the top at 11,158 feet of elevation. The highway incline goes as steep as a 7 percent grade. This is the maximum grade allowed on any Interstate across the country. Doesn't this sound like the making for a great truck torture test? The Ike Gauntlet was born. Of course, "Ike" was President Eisenhower's nickname.

The idea behind Ike Gauntlet is simple. Load a truck and trailer close to the truck's maximum Gross Combination Weight Rating (GCWR), and run it up and down the Ike Gauntlet highway. Diminished air density near the top of the test robs a naturally aspirated engine of a third of its power. Any engine and transmission will be taxed to the maximum on this grade.

One of the dangers of driving on steep roads

The trucks must be safe and practical on the way down. This is a test of a truck's stopping and load-handling abilities. The ability to stop a heavy load on the way down is more important than pulling it up the mountain. A truck's transmission and brakes are put to the ultimate test here.

The measurement is simple. The trucks must maintain a safe and practical speed at or below the 60 MPH speed limit on the way down. Going westbound on I-70, we exit the tunnel at 50 MPH. The trucks are using Tow/Haul mode with exhaust brakes enabled (if so equipped).

The point is to remove the driver's skill from the test. The driver is not shifting the transmission manually. (Note: All of the trucks we have tested over the last several years were equipped with an automatic transmission.) The driver allows the truck to accelerate naturally down the hill. If the truck and trailer go over the speed limit of 60 MPH, the driver applies the brake firmly (not slamming on it) in order to bring the truck back down to 50 MPH. If required, the brake application procedure is repeated until the eight miles of downhill are completed.

Some trucks require one or a few brake applications. These are the trucks that have especially smart "grade shifting" algorithms in their transmissions, and all systems, including the brakes, work at their best. Some trucks require ten or more brake applications. These systems require more work. The goal is to have the least number of brake applications as to not overheat and wear them out. There are two runaway truck ramps on this stretch of I-70 that serve as a constant reminder of the downhill danger. We monitor transmission and engine temperatures on all runs. Transmissions can heat up as they work hard on the way down.

Ike Gauntlet: The Way Up

A truck's engine and transmission will be stressed to the maximum, gaining more than 2,300 feet of elevation over just eight miles. The maximum grade of the climb is 7 percent. The engine will be starving for oxygen and struggling to make power at the finish line, which is 11,158 feet above sea level. The test is to use maximum throttle input on the way up in order to maintain the 60 MPH speed limit (or the maximum speed the truck is able to maintain). The driver makes his or her best effort to not go over the 60 MPH speed limit. Cruise control systems do not work under these wide open throttle conditions. This is a serious test for the driver, as very slow moving semi-trucks and other vehicles are obstacles to maintaining momentum and staying at or near 60 MPH.

We reset each truck's trip computer at the start of the test. We time each run up the mountain and record the trip's MPG as reported by the truck's computer.

At the end, each truck is scored on a scale of 100 points. The Ike Gauntlet scoring system allows a maximum score of 25 points for the downhill section, uphill time, uphill MPG, and average subjective score. The truck loses one point for each brake application on the way down. The benchmark time up the hill is eight minutes. Every five seconds over the benchmark time subtracts a point from the truck's overall score. The truck cannot gain points for going under eight minutes. The benchmark MPG number is 6.0 MPG. Every 0.2 MPG below that, and the truck loses a point. The truck can gain points for doing better than 6.0 MPG.

2016 Ram 1500 and Ram 3500 HD Dually

The Ike Gauntlet test is extreme and may seem unreasonable to some. It is a challenge that many truck owners and truckers/transporters must deal with on a regular basis. If a truck does well towing on the Ike Gauntlet, you know you have an excellent towing machine, no matter where you live.

How Does Elevation Affect Horsepower?

We are based in Colorado, just north of Denver. We have easy access to the Rocky Mountains, be it a challenging off-road trail or the difficult Ike Gauntlet towing test. Still, we must deal with the negative effect of high elevation every day. You may not be worried about high altitude where you live, but you still need to consider negative effects of high humidity and hot temperatures.

An internal combustion engine is an air pump at its core. It sucks in air and the oxygen in it, adds fuel, makes power, and spits the remains back out as exhaust. Altitude, relative humidity, and ambient temperature are the three factors that can combine to kill horsepower and torque that your engine produces. You want to haul and tow a lot with your truck, and every horsepower and pound-foot of torque matter when you load up near the limits.

Should you care about this? If it's a nice 70F° morning with relatively low humidity and you are at sea level, then no. However, a hot summer day and high humidity will have a noticeable effect on acceleration and grade climbing ability, especially when your air conditioning is set on full blast.

The SAE provides standards by which trucks, and all vehicles in general, are measured against. The SAE J1349 standard (revision June 1990) provides a formula to calculate relative horsepower for naturally aspirated engines.

Turbocharged and supercharged engines, especially those with intercoolers, help alleviate negative effects of your surrounding environment. However, all turbochargers and superchargers are not created equal. Some are more efficient than others, but none are able to give you all 100 percent of power in heat or at high altitude. Thus, this formula only applies to naturally aspirated engines.

You can easily find relative horsepower calculators on the Internet. Just get the relative barometric pressure (measured in inches Hg/Mercury) and relative humidity percentage (percent) using your favorite weather information provider. You also need the current ambient temperature (degrees Fahrenheit) and the elevation (feet). Get these four numbers plugged into a calculator, and you get the percent of horsepower you are currently producing.

For example, our test track is located at 5,200 feet above sea level. Consider a barometric pressure of 30.08 in Hg, relative humidity of 25 percent, and temperature of 72F° – the truck being tested produces only 82.4 percent of its rated horsepower. The big bad 6.2-liter EcoTec3 V8 in your GM pickup truck that is rated at 420 horsepower and 460 pound-foot of torque is making about 346 horses and 379 pound-foot of twist at our test track.

Okay, so you don't live north of Denver, Colorado. How about Dallas, Texas? Elevation near downtown is 430 feet. A typical June day could bring a temperature of 95F°, relative humidity of 89 percent, and barometric pressure of 29.96 in Hg. Your truck is making 93.4 percent of its power on that day. That same 6.2-liter V8 is now at 392 horsepower and 430 pound-foot of torque.

Naturally aspirated engines at the top of the Ike Gauntlet are losing about a third of their standard power rating. That big GM V8 is making 279 horsepower and 305 pound-foot of torque up there.

TOWING HIGHWAY MPG: THE DAILY GRIND

The extreme Ike Gauntlet test is all well and good, but what about a more real-life example of how a truck performs? How does the truck do at the daily grind? Enter the towing highway MPG test! Why perform a towing MPG test on the highway?

Many truck owners spend time towing a trailer on a highway. They might be pulling a U-Haul trailer across country, hauling an equipment/supplies trailer to a job site, taking a camping trailer to the next adventure, or towing a boat for a relaxing day on the lake. People like Mr. Truck tow horses or livestock! Towing on a highway is something most of us can relate to.

Any meaningful test requires control of the environment. We picked a highway loop that measures precisely 98 miles on the Interstate I-76 northeast of Denver, Colorado. This stretch is not heavily traveled and the highway itself is relatively flat. It's about as flat as an Interstate can get in Colorado.

2016 Toyota Tundra TRD Pro

We leave the truck stop and go forty-nine miles in one direction, and then return the forty-nine miles back to the same fueling station. We use cruise control set at 70 MPH for all runs. Although this stretch of the highway has a 75 MPH speed limit, we run all highway MPG tests at 70 MPH. This allows us a better margin of safety, as this stretch of highway can get windy.

The EPA rates midsize and light-duty (aka half-ton) trucks for city, highway, and combined MPGs, but they do not give a rating for trucks when towing a trailer or for heavy-duty pickups. This is where we come in.

We use a "double-click" method to top off the fuel tank before each run. We let the pump click the first time, we wait thirty seconds, and then manually add fuel until the pump clicks and stops for the second time. We use the same fill-up method when we return to the same pump after ninety-eight miles on the highway. We calculate the real-world MPG and also compare the results with the reading from the truck's trip computer. The two results almost never match exactly. The number we finally report is the calculated number, based on the gallons filled at the pump.

When towing, we always use the truck's Tow/Haul mode, although this does not significantly affect the results. Tow/Haul mode transmission shift logic does not really kick in at 70 MPH. We always use manufacturer recommended fuel and/or octane specification. We run all tests in 2WD mode. We do not perform tests during high winds, rain, or snow.

GOLD MINE HILL AND CLIFFHANGER: HIGH MOUNTAIN OFF-ROADING

Your truck is a symbol of freedom, and off-road capability is a big part of the equation. This is why we use two challenging trails in the Rocky Mountains near Boulder, Colorado to evaluate a truck's off-road worthiness.

2016 Nissan Titan XD PRO-4X

The Gold Mine Hill is a moderately challenging trail. It is accessible year-round, but it may become impassable in the winter when the snow gets too deep. The trail is so called because it leads up to a defunct gold mine that was active in the nineteenth and the early twentieth centuries. This off-road challenge consists of three stages. First is a steep and rocky incline that is closely lined by trees. This is just a warm-up. The second is a 90-degree left turn that is part of the incline. We always come to a complete stop before the turn to kill the momentum and make it more difficult. This is a place where the truck's 4x4 or AWD system is really put to the test as weight is shifted while navigating this tight turn. This is where tire choice becomes paramount. Finally, a steeper and washed-out section with large dips is there to test every aspect of the truck's off-road performance, including: ground clearance, approach/departure/breakover angles, suspension articulation, and tire grip. The passenger front tire lits off the ground on most trucks that attempt the final stage. Trucks that don't have off-road oriented or specialized tires or a locking differential are not likely to make it to the top of Gold Mine Hill.

We use five criteria to evaluate each truck's off-road worthiness:

- **Tires**

- **Ground clearance, approach/departure/breakover angles**

- **AWD / 4x4 system traction management**

- **Suspension articulation and comfort**

- **Power delivery**

Some trucks make the Gold Mine Hill look easy. These are the trucks that are eligible for TFLtruck's Gold Hitch: Off-Road Truck of the Year Award. These trucks also graduate to the Cliffhanger trail test.

The Cliffhanger 2.0 is a new trail that we certified in 2016 for testing the most capable 4x4 trucks. The likes of the Ram Power Wagon, Toyota TRD Pro, and the Ford Raptor are the trucks eligible to tackle this trail.

The Cliffhanger is longer than the Gold Mine Hill and it goes above the tree line. The payoff is a special 360 degree view that features the Continental Divide to the west and the Front Range to the east. The way to get there is a steep and rock layden trail that requires maximum traction. There is not much warm-up time. Rocks the size of basketballs, and often larger, can quickly stop your progress. There is a medium-sized ledge halfway through the trail that requires maximum ground clearance and adequate underbody skid plate protection. It is possible for trucks with a longer wheelbase to touch a large rock underneath. Driver skill and spotter's help are required. This trail was certified with a 2016 Jeep Wrangler Rubicon Hard Rock.

MR. TRUCK

3

NEW vs. USED

TEN YEARS OF SELLING NEW AND USED TRUCKS

This is my favorite debate. I have been on both sides: bought dozens of used trucks and now I buy new, at least for this year.

Invoice, holdback, 3-4 percent back of invoice, rebates, 0 percent interest all mean a new truck could be $5,000 to $10,000 below MSRP (manufacturer's suggested retail price). Consider the opposite: a used truck that you have no clue whether the dealer took it in as trade or bought at auction thousands below blue book value. On a new truck you can calculate a good deal, but on used trucks you're shooting in the dark if you're buying from a dealer. If you can find a one-owner used truck that didn't tow, has all the maintenance records, and is at least two years old, you have a case for a used truck. We're all familiar with invoices on new trucks. Not all are real, but generally it gives you a starting place. Invoice minus holdback is what the dealer pays, which is 3 percent to 4 percent off the invoice. A new truck dealer may get other incentives if they sell their monthly quota. After subtracting whatever the current rebate is, all you have to try to negotiate is the D&H (dealer handling). Fleet departments don't charge D&H, but it's hard to get the retail side of a dealership to let it go. I'm not against used trucks; most of mine have started out used when I bought them. If your budget points you to an older truck, then you'll want to read Chapter 6 on "Used Truck Judging 101."

We have all heard how much you lose when you drive a new car off the lot. The people you hear saying this the most are the USED CAR SALESMEN. Trucks and cars drop like a rock after you buy them whether they were used or new; that is the wholesale spread. Car dealers make more money on used trucks than new. You don't have an invoice on used vehicles, and you have no way of knowing exactly how much the dealer paid for it. Very few people pay full retail for new vehicles, and then there are those rebates. It would surprise you how close the actual sales price of a new vehicle and a one year old one are. And you know the new one wasn't raced to the airport by one hundred different people. I actually know people who trade-in every year and never change their oil.

Since trucks have better resale value and generally last longer than cars, they can be priced even higher at one year old than new. I have seen that happen often. To see a significant difference, you need to go back three years in trucks. Crew cab 4x4s are the kings on resale value. In 4x4s, used can be a whole new experience. Since you won't know how much off-road use it had, a 4x4 can create its own payment! It seems that every part on the bottom of a 4x4 truck costs over $2,000. If you are the first owner of a truck—especially a 4x4 or diesel—and you take care of it, it can last you decades for less cost per mile.

Did the used truck tow big loads often? What do you know about the truck history? Or should you buy new and know what the truck did in its past life?

Top Five Reasons to Buy
a New Truck

1. It's all new: A new truck has new everything. All you have to worry about is making the payment. The interior is spotless, exterior has no dents and is all the same color. New tires, new brakes, an engine that doesn't use oil, and it's quiet inside the cab. A used truck, especially older than three years, could have a dozen owners. It's kind of like marrying someone that was married six times before; makes you think about all the previous users. Not all owners handle maintenance the same, or use the same oil brand or chase coyotes through the same river. Then there are the states that use salt on their roads in the winter, or worse, use magnesium chloride, which eats metal and plastic on your truck. Eastern state owners may drive in the rain every day, Southwestern drivers might

let the truck sit in the sun (120 degrees Fahrenheit) for months and crack the paint, curl the plastic grill, or dry rot the tires.

2. Lower payments: At 0 percent interest or even 3 percent, new trucks are easier to finance. Truck manufacturers offer the lowest interest on loans or give you bigger rebates if you finance yourself, with sometimes a combination of the two. My new truck financed at 1.9 percent with big rebates; my car financed at 0 percent interest with nothing down for six years. It's like free money. Now look at financing a used truck: the term will be shorter and the interest will be higher depending on your credit. Now, an average interest on a used truck can be 5 percent or higher, with no rebates and maybe no factory warranty left. If payments are important to you like they are to me, that is the big difference between new and used. If the prices are close, then rebates and lower interest are important. A new truck payment can be more than a $100 a month lower.

3. Known history: You know how your new truck is used. You know when you changed the oil. You know how big your trailer is. On a used truck, you don't know how many people raced it, or how fast or slow they drove (both can hurt it). On a used truck, you don't know if it came from the last hurricane with rust on the starter, mold under the carpet, new paint, and water in the tail lights. If the truck you're looking at has a drop-in bedliner, look under it. That's an old trick: to put in a bedliner so you don't see the gooseneck ball or bed rust. I know many used dealers who take the receiver hitches off so you don't think it was used for trailering.

4. Warranty and roadside assistance: Imagine not having to work on your used truck on weekends. I used to do that; every weekend I was working on the vehicles or the house. With the forty-plus computers on your truck, just plugging a mechanic's computer into your truck will cost at least $80. And, if you don't have the right computer you may not even be able to work on the newer trucks yourself.

5. Long cross-country vacations: To take the family on the road, you need a dependable truck towing your RV. Anything can happen to a used truck. When I was young, alternators, starters, and spark plugs needed frequent changing. Breakdowns on the road cost twice what they do when you're close to home, but trucks are more dependable now. That's why I started buying new, so I wouldn't worry about my family breaking down on the road when I was several states away.

Top Five Reasons to Buy a Used Truck

1. Total price: If the truck is at least three years old, the cash price should be dramatically lower than a new truck. On a used truck, you can look up its history with the VIN number at that brand's service center. Recalls will be there, dealer repairs will be there, and on Carfax you can look up accident reports. You can read reviews done on the truck years ago, and truck forums will give you insight into other owners' experience with trucks you're considering buying.

2. Lower sales tax: The lower the cost of the used truck, the lower the sales tax. Generally, license plates cost less on a used truck. Generally, insurance is lower on a used truck. Same with parts for your used truck: after a few years, the parts are all available at the parts stores, like NAPA, O'Reilly Autozone, etc., which generally are cheaper than a truck brand parts counter.

3. Your neighbors won't think you're rich: If you're driving a new $90,000 truck, you'll be surprised at all the friends and relatives who will want to borrow money from you. Warren Buffet and Sam Walton drove used trucks for a reason. If people think you have money, it bothers them.

4. You can crank up the power: Once the factory warranty is expired, you can add all the power modules, headers, and nitro, not having to worry about voiding any factory warranties. This is important to those of you who hop into your used diesel for the weekend drag race at the track, or pull sleds at the county fair. If you like to modify your truck's suspension for radical off-road use, then an older used truck is up your alley.

5. Trucks last: Just like the Energizer Bunny, if you don't drive long distances or are a volunteer fireman, you can keep a truck for decades. I have a forty-six-year-old truck. On my farm, most of my vehicles are at least thirty years old. And because they cost less, you can buy several trucks. Every American should have a truck collection.

A truck can last decades, long after the monthly payment. Buying a used truck means payments for less years. Customize it and make it part of the family. My 1970 Chevy C10 is mechanically sound;

it just needs some new paint and a little sheet metal. An average truck passes through many owners. Sometimes they are passed down for generations. You can build your collection faster with used trucks.

2016 GMC Sierra HD and 2002 Chevrolet Silverado HD

As with everything, knowledge or lack of knowledge can influence your truck purchase. One thing a lot of folks don't understand is the Consumer Protection Act, which gives you three days to think over the new mortgage on your house, or a loan on the new Kirby vacuum that was just demonstrated on your carpet. If you leave your home and go to a dealership, you don't have three days to change your mind on the purchase contract. The law was designed to keep consumers from being pressured on important loans or being talked into buying something by the traveling salesman coming to your home. But leave the house and you're committed when you sign on the dotted line.

FIRST YEAR MODEL TRUCK BLUES

The year 2003 has turned out to be a dramatic example of "first year blues." The Ford 6.0L Power Stroke trucks I drove for two years were great, and I thought '03 would be a great year for Ford. But that's the underlying risk of the first year of dramatic change. Ford Super Duties for 2003 had a new diesel engine. Engineers and developers created a new engine, and then the corporation accountants (bean counters) got hold of it and slashed part of the component of the engine system to save money. I've driven and pulled with ones that are great and ones with problems. When Sturman Industries designed the G2 injector for the 6.0L Power Stroke and the International VT365, it was great. It had a pre-shot (pilot injection), two compression shots, and post shot. And then the accountants started deleting components to lower the cost. I've interviewed Blue Diamond engineers (Ford and International) who made the Ford F650 and F750 Mexico and International manufactured 6.0L Power Stroke. They knew the problems were coming with the 6.0L. The engine was well-made, but problems occurred with EGR coolers, head gaskets, injectors, the control module, and the list goes on. This relates to first year blues on new models with several new components.

On the other hand, Dodge in '03 changed the diesel, transmission, frame, axles, transfer case, suspension, steering, etc. That many changes created a risk of the first year blues, but they came out a champion with few problems. The year 2003 was surprising. This is back when Daimler owned Dodge. Hemi was reintroduced in the Dodge 1500 and their trucks did well. So the first year blues didn't apply to the Dodge trucks in 2003.

More recent first year trucks include: the 2015 Ford F150, 2017 Ford Super Duty, 2017 Honda Ridgeline, 2016 Titan XD, 2016 Toyota Tacoma, and 2015 Colorado and Canyon. Do your research.

I know you've heard it before, but we all give into our emotions. The new model looks so cool, you just have to have it! I've seen, bought, and sold first year models. As hard as the manufacturers try to get the bugs out, trucks are very complicated products. It sometimes takes thousands of vehicles in use to find the weak links. Sure, they give recalls when most things are discovered, but how many trips to the shop do you have time for? The press releases and reviews you see before and at the introduction of a new truck are usually from the manufacturers, and do you think they are objective? You're the one stuck with the payments and downtime, don't be the guinea pig, too. GM's first year Duramax diesel had problems, but 2002 was much better. So on a used truck, do your research, Google "first year" for the truck you're looking at, and check the truck forums to see what owners are saying about their first year model trucks.

GAS VS. DIESEL

I like new diesels; used diesels can mean a hefty repair bill. If you are a mechanic, buy anything you want. But for instance, injectors on a GM Duramax can cost thousands after the warranty runs out. Usually after 130,000 miles, injectors can go. Diesel transmissions can be an unbelievable expense. New diesel trucks generally have a five year 100,000 mile drivetrain warranty. Gas trucks may only have a three year 36,000 mile warranty. Diesel mechanics charge more per hour. Oil changes cost more. We cover the rest of the story in Chapter 7.

If you are looking at a gas engine, there are very little differences in price between half-tons and HD three-quarter tons, but you get more choices with transmissions and axle ratio's in HD three-quarter ton trucks. HD three-quarter ton trucks have a full floating axle, with twice as many bearings in the rear axle, and are designed to be loaded all the time with heavier springs, frames, shocks, tire ratings, etc. Even the way they ride has changed dramatically in the last five years. In the old days, a three-quarter ton truck rode like a basketball and needed some weight in the bed to ride better.

With used trucks, be careful with the light-duty three-quarter tons, because there are half-tons with more wheel bolts, and it's not easy to tell them apart. If you want a diesel, then there are more factors to consider. Trucks can be confusing, and most people end up asking their truck salesperson important questions. Often the salesperson does not know the answers because they just started selling yesterday or last week. So they just make something up and "TO" (turn you over to a manager who will smoothly tell you anything you want to hear).

Very few managers in the auto business know anything about trucks; they just know how to smile and manipulate you with, "What can I do to earn your business today?" and, "Sure that truck will pull your trailer, my brother-in-law pulls his with that exact truck."

I suggest you get an owner's manual after you buy your used truck to know what the recommended service schedules are. Helm is a good place to order your manual. It's where dealers order theirs.

Truck Brands

When it comes to recommending the best truck, everyone has their opinion and few of us humans let facts get in our way. When I was growing up, my dad had a model 92 Massey combine and my uncle had a John Deere model 95. And of course we thought the Massey had to be the best combine around. Then a funny thing happened. I ended up helping my uncle harvest wheat one summer. I couldn't believe how easy the John Deere was to grease and work on. Everything you worked on was on the outside where you could get to it. The Massey had everything buried on the inside. Since you always have to work on combines, I was impressed. But you know, I never could convince my dad to buy a John Deere! That's how trucks are. If your grandpa has a Dodge truck, your dad, your brother and your cousins all have Dodge trucks, not much chance you'll buy a Ford. This is why Toyota Tundra and Nissan Titan have so much trouble capturing market share. Brand loyalty is a powerful force. We become brand-blind.

Truck brands keep improving, and if you get the latest model (after their first year), you will like it much better than your old model. Do yourself a favor: when you need a truck, look at all the brands. I did an article for *Turbo Diesel Register* magazine. They are the big Dodge/Ram diesel magazine. My assignment was to write an article on "why you don't want to buy a Dodge Diesel truck." The editor wanted readers to look at options and not be brand-blind.

I like competition in diesel trucks and it's closer than it has ever been, with GM and Ford improving their diesels and Dodge improving its body and transmission. So all three are very close; actually, the closest these brands have ever been. Ram Heavy-duty just passed GM in sales numbers on diesels after GM passed Ram a few years ago with the Duramax. But Ford, which has out-sold Dodge and GM diesels combined for over a decade, is still #1 in sales by a wide margin. This means you find more used Ford trucks. If you think you need the best truck every other year, get a two year lease and keep switching brands.

We cover more on this in Chapter 7, but it's important when deciding between used and new trucks. I've updated the time it takes to pay for a diesel engine option with fuel savings from 80,000 miles to 150,000 miles. Calculate how long it takes to pay for the extra $8,000 to $11,000 for the diesel option with fuel savings. It's easy to get addicted to the power of a diesel. If you tow large trailers or keep a truck forever, the diesel option makes sense. But if you trade trucks every three years and don't need the capacity, you may not have paid for the extra cost of a diesel engine, special transmission, more expensive oil changes, and fuel filter changes, from the extra fuel savings of the diesel option.

A used diesel not maintained properly and over-trailered beyond its factory weight ratings can be an expensive time bomb. Diesel mechanics charge more than gas engine mechanics per hour. Engines, radiators, alternators, starters, batteries, etc., all cost more in diesel trucks. But a used diesel truck with a pedigree from a one-owner, pulling moderate trailer weights and with service receipts is worth a premium. Some truck owners use the high setting on power chips and micro turners, which works them hard to have most of the goody used up. That's how most of my trucks were when I was done. I stripped them down to the frame and sold them by the pound. Trucks can last several decades, and so can the wrong choice.

Comparing Trucks

I believe in long test drives and several of them. Used salespeople will try to have you to turn right four times to get you back to the dealership fast; "right turn Clyde" if you remember Clint Eastwood's *Every Which Way But Loose*. Always remember it's your money and you are in control. If the salesperson doesn't want to accept those terms, then I use a borrowed phrase from Amway: "Some will, some won't, so what, next!"

Always remember to get your money first. You can always take zero percent interest from the manufacture financing when available, but be prepared with your own options. Before you get talked into the dealer extended warranties, do your own research. Sometimes your credit union or insurance companies have better warranties. Keep checking back on the latest rebates, recalls and interest rates, which can change each month. There are crash tests from the National Highway Traffic Safety Administration available at http://www.nhtsa.gov/. And also at https://www.fueleconomy.gov. is a nice VIN lookup section and information on EPA mileage for trucks that are 8500 GVWR and lower.

One way to look at buying a truck new or used is to consider your future needs. The month I got out of the business, my oldest son rolled his truck and we had to go truck shopping. I had forgotten how hard it was. We started out going dealer to dealer, reading the paper, looking on the Internet, and I just tagged along as dumb ol' dad playing with my granddaughter. After my son and daughter-in-law got tired of it, and after changing their minds several times on which vehicle they wanted, they asked for help. I got on the cell phone and called one of the veteran salespeople I bought from and trusted as a broker. I told him what I needed and then we went and picked it up.

Of course I have the advantage, knowing the dealer cost of vehicles and who to trust. But the point I was trying to make to my kids was: you're going to buy a lot of vehicles over your lifetime. Find the salesperson and dealer you trust, build a relationship and send them your friends. You still need to do price research to keep everyone honest. It's natural for a salesperson on commission to want to make more money. I would think a positive relationship with a dealer you trust would take some of the stress out of something you will do often for the rest of your life.

We are all trying to feed our families, and I don't expect people to work for free. But that's just me: the older I get the more I can see both sides of any argument.

Should you buy your truck from a new dealer or a used dealer?

There are several great used car lots, ones that have been in families for generations. And there are several that are high pressure, and target you for one big sale. I've known used lots that send buyers all over the country to buy the last flood, hurricane, hail, or tornado-damaged vehicles at auctions, and ship them home to be repainted and rebuilt. Ever wonder how used lots have the latest model year vehicles? Manufacturers also sell the lemons they can't fix at those auctions. Watch out for the newer models with low miles, thinking there is still factory warranty left. They don't all have it.

I've known a lot of car salesman in my ten years of being in the business. They make more money working for the used lots. The problem with new lots, the big ones with the most inventory, is that they have the most "new green pea salespeople" who naturally don't know much about trucks. What do you do? I suggest you do your own homework. Go to the manufacturer's websites. New dealers have the manufacturer behind them on new, and also usually on the used inventory. With the factory-certified mechanics close by, it's easier to have the vehicle checked out. If the vehicle you are looking at is the same brand they sell new, it can be traced on the factory computer for recalls and repair history. And you can find out if there really is factory warranty left!

Used lots of ill repute will watch you drive away hoping to not see you again. They will not be your friend when the truck breaks down. If the new dealer is well-established, they have considerably more invested in their franchise than the used lot with a two year lease on their property. The better auctions that sell the factory program cars from the manufactories, lease returns, and executive cars, usually sell these vehicles to the franchise dealers first at special monthly auctions. Guess who the auctions sell the lemons and worn-out trade-ins to? We know that there are both good and bad new and used vehicle dealers. But, since prices are usually comparable between the two, you need to decide which one gets your future sales and service business? If you find unbelievable deals somewhere, what does common sense say?

MR. TRUCK

4

HOW TO MATCH YOUR TRUCK TO YOUR TRAILER & VICE VERSA

OR

PROPER COPULATING A TRUCK & TRAILER WITH TRUCK CLASSES EXPLAINED

A TRUCK AND A TRAILER GET HITCHED

The number one cause of trailer accidents is the wrong size ball. I know you guys reading this know how big your balls are. Pickup truck and trailer compatibility is in your control. What guidelines make the union between your truck and trailer long-lasting and safe for your family?

Rules for towing and trailers in general are less-regulated in the US. In Canada, you have to have your trailer inspected each year, and your brake-away system uses a full size battery. In Europe, trailers have to be tested on a track before they can be sold. In Australia, trailers over 10,000 pounds are required to have air brakes on the trailer and all goosenecks use three inch balls which were implemented in the US on 30,001 pound trailers and larger in the last five years.

The SAE makes up the requirements for trailers but has no enforcement authority. The DOT (Department of Transportation) has a few trailer requirements but mostly it governs semi-trailers. For example, since 1991 over-the-road semi-trailers have been required to have an ABS (anti lock braking system) and a side light to tell you if the trailer ABS is working. On your horse trailer, RV, or car trailer, you still aren't required to have ABS brakes. DOT, EPA, and SAE have an extreme impact on your truck's manufacturing requirements.

Gather all the information you can on your truck's capacity. Most trailer towing, payload, tongue weight, and axle weight ratings will be on the truck manufacturer's website, but you have to dig into the websites. First, you have to know your truck configuration. The more options on your truck, the lower the payload and trailer capacity. So a stripped down 4x2 single cab truck with a gas engine will have a higher payload than a 4x4 crew-cab long-bed diesel, even though we all know a typical diesel engine has more power and torque to tow trailers than a gas engine. Don't forget braking, including the diesel exhaust brake. The extra weight of a loaded diesel truck can be better at controlling a trailer. So what do you do: buy a less powerful gas truck that fits the requirements including insurance and warranty, or buy a diesel that will make it to the top of the mountain with ease? Here are the rules, and you can decide.

If you're buying a new truck, get the trailer tow package, including: integrated trailer brake controller, receiver hitch, larger radiator, and transmission cooler. If you bought a used truck, take the VIN number to that brand's service center to see what options the truck came with. Some of the codes are on the door of the glove box, and the Truck Safety Compliance Certification is on the inside of the driver's side door with codes for axle ratio, limited slip, as well as the tire pressure recommended by the truck manufacturer. Confused yet? Don't worry, that's why we're "truck nuts." We will help you with the "truth about trucks and trailers."

GCWR is a truck plus loaded trailer for a maximum rating. Truck manufacturers subtrac the truck's curb weight from GCWR for an approximation of the truck's maximum towing capacity. The real world formula is GCWR minus what your truck really weighs with the cargo it carries, passengers, and fuel for the real allowable maximum trailer weight. The weight will work for static loads in your trailer like hay or cars or gold. For animals like horses, my rule of thumb is 15 percent less trailer load. Big animals move around swatting flies with their tails, and have a higher center of gravity.

Now that you know your maximum trailer weight, next is your payload. Payload isn't just what goes in your truck bed, it's also the trailer tongue weight, passengers, the 45 cal. under your seat, and tools in your box. Payload is important, and many trucks have too low of a max payload capacity to use its maximum trailer weight. Payload is important for towing trailers. Bumpers that pull trailers over 5,000 pounds at 10 percent tongue weight need Weight Distributing Hitches with built-in sway control. Newer duallys have more payload capability, which allows heavier trailers. Too many trucks don't have enough payload capacity. The simple formula for payload is GVWR minus CW (curb weight) equals PL (payload).

It is important to remember that after you figure what your trailer weighs loaded, generally a bumper pull tongue weight will be 10 to 15 percent on a balanced trailer and 15 to 25 percent for a gooseneck/mini 5th-wheel tongue weight. The catch is the tongue weight comes off your truck's payload. Now with that number, do you have enough left for passengers? Sometimes not, which seems to be a trend with truck manufacturers. New trucks will have a high trailer weight capacity, but with a tongue weight that won't let you ever reach that big trailer number. Unless, of course, you don't have passengers and the driver only weighs 100 pounds. My left leg weighs 100 pounds.

Weigh-Safe tongue weight scale

Tongue weight: do you know yours? Did you weigh your truck and trailer? After you know what your loaded trailer weighs, now what's the tongue weight? Weigh-Safe has a billet aluminum adjustable receiver hitch, but it has a built-in scale. Now you can know your tongue weight each time you tow.

Enter the SAE J2807 (Society of Automotive Engineers) to save us. The SAE J2807 standard started in 2008 to help judge real truck capacity instead of marketing with all the extreme ads. But like Congress, a good idea doesn't make it without being diluted to a useless guideline. It is not a totally useless SAE standard, but watered down in favor of truck manufacturers who make up the committee that votes on it. Some trailer manufacturers and hitch companies are also on the committee, but the most influence is from the truck side; like the fox put in charge of the hen house. I agreed with most of the initial J2807 guidelines, with 20 percent tongue weight for gooseneck/fifth wheel trailers. Then it was changed to 15 percent tongue weight. But it's still a guideline and not a law. So 15 percent on a gooseneck can be 20 percent. If road conditions are bad, the extra tongue weight on a gooseneck is safer. I followed a dually with a light tongue and watched him roll off the road on snow. Semi-trucks have 40 percent or more tongue weight and do better on ice. Traction comes from weight and good tires. We try to follow J2807 guidelines reviewing trucks, but if the weather is bad, I recommend 20 percent or more for control.

The rest of SAE J2807 is helpful when comparing trucks' towing capacity and a whole lot better than watching new truck ads on TV.

Summary of the Rules:

1) Cooling capability towing a trailer on a twelve-mile highway upgrade near Davis Dam in Arizona with temperature near 100 degrees.

2) Launch and acceleration performance on a level road and a 12 percent upgrade with a trailer.

3) Combined handling performance—understeer, oversteer and trailer sway.

4) Combined braking performance—stopping distance and parking brake-hold on grade.

5) Structural performance for the vehicle and hitch or hitch receiver, which includes up to 70 pounds of aftermarket hitch equipment.

6) Testing with both a driver and passenger in the vehicle, each weighing 150 pounds on trucks under 8,500 pounds. GVWR. An extra 100 pounds included on heavier trucks.

All this delivers the GCWR and TW (trailer weight) you can use to compare trucks. Dually's are given more time in these tests. You can find all the details at http://www.sae.org/. Manufacturers didn't all comply the same year. Toyota was the first to implement it on new trucks, and Ford was the last. When you are test driving new trucks, ask about the SAE J2807 guidelines and if the truck you are looking at is compliant. This information is not easy to find, but you can always use this book or TFLtruck.com and MrTruck. com reviews to help you decide. If the truck is compliant it had to meet the criteria. This will help you judge trucks.

A receiver hitch extension like this one will lower your tongue capacity by a third. It has leverage.

Another important aspect of payload concerns slide-in truck campers. Hard side campers can weigh over 4,000 pounds. In other words, all of your payload capacity giving you nothing left for trailer tongue weight. One option can be a lighter popup slide-in camper. Take the weight of your loaded camper, subtract it from your truck's payload including passengers, and see what weight is left to use as trailer tongue weight. Don't expect this combination of camper and trailer to work well on a half-ton truck. This is why you often see dually trucks carrying big truck campers in their beds.

The picture on the next page shows why folks want to use a hitch extension. Large slide-in campers can stick out three feet past the truck bed.

The last capacity number you need to know is, front and rear axle maximum weight set by manufacturer or the (GAWR) Gross Axle Weight Rating. The rear GAWR is the most important; not exceeding the payload rating will keep you under rear GAWR.

The axle gear ratio refers to the relationship between the engine RPM and rear axle rotation. If you jack up the rear of your truck, mark the drive shaft, mark the outside of the tire, and put the engine at direct drive, the engine (drive shaft) rolls over 4.1 times and the rear wheel rotates once. That's a 4.10 axle ratio, which is a low gearing setup for towing up grades, starting from a standstill and holding the engine in higher RPMs. All making it a good towing axle, but limiting top speed and efficiency. That's changing too; with new 10-speed automatic transmissions, first gear can be lower and gear spacing closer, making the traditional low (4.10) axle ratio not necessary. This will change axle ratio final drives to better fuel mileage gears, like 3.2 or even into the 2's. Semi-trucks have already done this with 18, 14, 13, and 12-speed transmissions with 3.55 and 3.73 final drive ratio at the axle.

As of this writing, towing gear-axle ratios for half-ton trucks are: GM 1500- 3.42, Ford F150- 3.73, Ram 1500- 3.92, and Toyota Tundra 4.30, in-between truck class Nissan Titan XD has a 3.92 ratio on diesel and 3.36 on the gas engine. Three-quarter ton and one-ton heavy-duty trucks are generally 3.42, 3.55, 3.73, and 4.10 axle ratios. However, the Ford F-450 class 3 truck has a 4.30 rear-end.

Do you wonder why manual transmissions have become extinct? Now you can't find manual transmissions in trucks outside the smallest horsepower Cummins diesel Ram heavy-duty and the midsize trucks. I kept this in the book because trucks last forever, and you might be looking for a used truck. A manual transmission used to sell the best behind a diesel. When I was selling trucks, you couldn't talk a person from the mountains into an auto tranny. They wanted the control of a stick and the ability to down shift and save the brakes going downhill. This was before exhaust brakes and tow/haul mode.

Back then automatic transmissions were rated to pull 3,000 pounds, or more than a manual transmission. The reason being, the asbestos is gone from the clutch, which improved the friction qualities; also the auto trannies have a lockup torque converter that locks up mechanically like a clutch and pressure plate behind a manual transmission. And, the torque converter stator doubles the torque coming from the flywheel with an auto. The computers now determine when the automatic shifts instead of a human making that decision. Knowing when to shift is important for pulling a trailer, getting better fuel mileage, and getting longer life from your engine. When your truck is new, the warranty will cover your auto transmission, but it will not replace your clutch after the first year. If I was driving in the mountains pulling a large trailer most of the time, I would use a manual transmission with a diesel. I like having all the gears I can find when coming down the mountain. On the other hand, if you were not experienced at downshifting a manual tranny on the fast side of the mountain, the automatic should be your choice.

Extendable and power-folding towing mirror with lights

If you have the choice and tow often, get the factory tow mirrors. If your trailer is 8.5 feet wide like my toy hauler, you need all the mirror extension you can find. Adjust your outside mirrors with each trailer. If you don't have a spotter or convex smaller mirrors built into your trailer mirrors, add them. The convex mirror can show you how your trailer tires are doing and help find the end of your trailer when turning corners. I like both outside mirrors to be the same, especially for backing. I don't understand why they put those mirrors with the warning "objects may appear smaller." I throw them away and get normal mirrors where "objects are the real size."

I also use wireless cameras on the back of the trailer for backing and to see the little cars that follow too close. Towing trailers puts your oil change in the severe duty category in the owner's manual. For me, that means every 3,000 miles if it's mostly trailering miles. When towing, your engine runs hotter and oil needs to be changed more often, as will most all maintenance schedules. **Always read your truck owner's manual about maintenance when trailering and weight rating!**

wireless camera

Now for a tip to save your life. Bumper pull trailers are more prone to sway even with a good weight distribution. You can get cut off on the highway or hit a patch of ice on a curve. This can happen to a gooseneck, also. So the trick that truckers use is to use the manual lever on the trailer brake controller and accelerate if there's room. This will straighten out the snake. If you go into a sway or the trailer is sliding sideways, don't hit your truck brakes. That can increase the trailer sway, especially on ice. But if you push the manual override button or lever on your trailer brake controller and let just the trailer brakes slow you down, the rig should straighten out.

I do this on icy, curvy mountain roads. There is also a difference between trailer leaf springs vs. torsion springs with trailer sway. Leaf springs can reload trailer sway, and keep it swaying until you push the trailer brake. The key to getting back control of your trailer is to practice. Take your truck and trailer to a large deserted parking lot and practice just using your manual brake controller. Then you'll be ready for an emergency maneuver to avoid a wreck.

Trailering Rules of the Road

Rule 1: Don't buy a truck that is rated to tow a smaller trailer than you have planned. We get talked into things. A salesperson's job is to sell you the smallest truck for the greatest price. But, you don't want to buy a truck just for it's MPG. Gas will seem cheap when you overheat your new truck or burn the brakes off your trailer on the first mountain road on your family vacation. As we discussed in the last chapter, the wrong truck can last a long time, too, and it's easier to make that monthly payment if you enjoy your truck.

Rule 2: Keep trailer and truck as level as possible. A level trailer has more effective brakes. With torsion axles, if one axle is dramatically higher, it can lock up when braking because there's not enough weight. Both truck and trailer will squat when loaded. If you can't be level, have the trailer tongue slightly down. A level rig will distribute your load on all the axle bearings.

Rule 3: Driving at night can help MPG because there's less wind and less traffic. Western states that always have wind usually have less wind at night, except for Kansas. This can give you an extra 3 MPG versus driving in a hard, side wind. There is less traffic at night, and you'll use A/C less. But if you don't feel comfortable driving at night or fear being broken down by yourself at night, don't do it.

Rule 4: Check tire pressure with a good truck gauge. I like steel valve stem extensions that you don't have to take the cap off to read. Tapping with a hammer on trailer tires to check air pressure is a myth. I know truckers do it, but my test with a hammer proved 40 PSI off from my trusty commercial air gauge.

Rule 5: Check the overall length of the truck and trailer, as some states only allow 65 or 70 feet. Call the DOT in the states where you'll be traveling. Nothing is worse than having to leave your trailer somewhere because you're over length.

Rule 6: Balance your trailer tires. Most aren't, but balanced tires can last 25-50 percent longer. All tires need to be balanced.

Rule 7: In the winter be aware of chain laws, especially if your truck is a 2-wheel drive. Some mountain passes even require chains on the trailer. In Colorado, it's a $1,000 fine for not carrying chains when you are towing commercially.

Rule 8: Carry extra trailer axle bearings, seals, and serpentine belt for the truck. Breakdowns on the road are expensive.

Rule 9: Learn to bypass interstates through large cities, as the main interstate may take you through all the rush hour traffic.

Rule 10: When you stop for fuel or snacks, feel your trailer wheels. If they are very hot, you may have a brake hanging up or a bearing going out.

Rule 11: I like using Slime or similar product on my trailer tires. The rear trailer tire catches a lot of nails from the front trailer tires.

Rule 12: Drive in the right lane when you can, not just because it's the slow lane, but because other drivers won't give you the proper room in front in the left lane. If you have to stop, sometimes you might need to brake on the right shoulder.

Rule 13: Safety chains are important. If something breaks so you're unhooked from the trailer, safety chains can give you some control as you use the trailer brake controller separately to get the trailer stopped. Crossing the safety chains allows the trailer coupler to drop into the chains and not hit the road. Make sure your jack is fully raised. If the trailer drops, safety chains can catch the trailer tongue and not have the jack dragging in the pavement.

Rule 14: You probably already know breakaway system batteries rarely last a year. Check them to see they are charged. If the police pull you over, they may test your trailer brakeaway cable. Leave the trailer lights on while driving so you'll know you have a connection and you should have trailer brakes.

Brakes: Stopping is more important than acceleration. That's why in the TFLtruck Ike Gauntlet, we count brake events coming down the mountain. Trucks have different speeds for tow/haul mode to grade shift to slow you down on the fast side of mountain roads. Newer trucks have proportional brakes to balance brake pressure between the front and rear axles. In my day, most of a truck's brake pressure was on the front axle, which meant when you added a trailer, it pushed down on the rear of the truck, lifting the front of the truck and lowering the truck's braking ability.

Short beds and short, short beds. The #1 selling truck in America is the short bed crew cab and has been for over ten years. Some half-ton trucks have 5.5 feet beds. Now try to hook that up to a gooseneck. The problem with short beds is the 90-degree jack-knife turning corners, but more so with backing up. Trailer manufacturers haven't heard of short bed trucks. I remember in the old days, some horse trailer dealers wouldn't sell you a trailer if you had a short bed truck. Now short bed trucks are called "standard beds." What a difference a couple of decades make. There are gooseneck and fifth wheel neck extensions to prevent knocking out your truck rear window.

Pictured below, shortbed half-ton truck towing a LITE mini fifth wheel trailer. Matched well for towing.

Which style bed hitch: gooseneck or mini fifth wheel?

The groups using the gooseneck hitches were farmers and ranchers, who didn't want a hitch to take up much space in the truck bed. They used the bed a lot for other things and they hooked up

their trailers often, so finding the "little ball" wasn't a concern. Another group was the retired snowbirds. Sometimes, after retiring it was the first time they owned a truck or pulled a trailer. And being retired, on fixed-income and somewhat conservative, this group liked something close to what semi-trucks had: a fifth wheel hitch. The mini fifth wheel was higher off the bed, so easier to see, and it looked stronger than the "little ball." And with a V-fork it took less experience to back up to the RV trailer.

I have pulled a lot of different trailers, and I remember how glad I was when I could afford to go from a bumper pull type trailer to a gooseneck. Fifth wheel or gooseneck trailers pull straight with very little "whip" if loaded correctly, compared to bumper types. And talk about backing a trailer. Bumper type trailers seem to react twice as fast as an easygoing, slow-reacting, "anybody could back-it" goose-neck trailer.

Road Trip Necessities

Lug nuts can loosen on your trailer. If you're lucky, the lug nuts will make a racket bouncing around in the hub cab so that you'll notice. On long trips, it's good to check trailer lug nuts with a star wrench, which tells you to tighten the lug nuts in a star pattern. Aluminum wheels can loosen up with contraction and expansion. Losing a trailer wheel happens more often than you think. All wheels used to be "stud pilot," meaning the wheel studs held the wheel load. Now trucks are "hub pilot," meaning the wheel load sits on the hub ring inside the bolt circle. But not trailers. We're still in the dark ages with weight on the studs, which can cause the lug nuts to loosen from driving. Get a torque wrench (mine cost $10). Your trailer/truck owner's manual will tell you how much to torque the lug nuts. While you are there, touch the wheel to see if it's overheated, which could mean a dragging brake or wheel bearings going out.

Trailer tire pressure is a daily check. Use the max PSI it says on the tire when cold (the truck or SUV will have a safety tag on the driver's door frame). Use these numbers instead of what is written on the tire. The truck manufacturer decides what is best; also, what it says in your truck/SUV owner's manual for your receiver hitch rating overrides what it says on the receiver hitch tag. Don't forget to keep an eye on all those tires for wear. You should not see the top of Lincoln's head on a penny in the groove on the face of the tires.

GLOSSARY

TERMINOLOGY FOR TRUCK & TRAILER CAPACITY

GVWR

Gross Vehicle Weight Rating—the maximum allowable weight of the fully-loaded vehicle with axles (including passengers and cargo). The GVW (gross vehicle weight) must never exceed the GVWR.

GAW

Gross Axle Weight—the total weight placed on each axle (front and rear), the rear being more important.

GAWR

Gross Axle Weight Rating—the maximum weight to be carried by a single axle (front or rear).

GCW

Gross Combination Weight—the weight of the loaded vehicle, (GVW) plus the weight of the fully loaded trailer.

GCWR

Gross Combination Weight Rating—the maximum allowable weight of the towing vehicle and the loaded trailer, including all cargo and passengers.

GTW

Gross Trailer Weight—the actual total weight of the loaded trailer. Trailer Gross Vehicle Weight not to exceed the GVWR of the trailer.

TW

Tongue Weight—refers to the amount of the trailer's weight that presses down on the trailer hitch, whether a bed mount hitch (mini fifth wheel or ball) or a receiver hitch attached at the rear of the truck.

WDH

Weight distributing hitch.

TRAILER AND RECEIVER HITCH CLASSES AND TYPES

Mounted to the truck's frame. The following ratings are the best combinations I can find. They seem to change year to year. Even the SAE ratings are hard to follow. Look in your truck's owner's manual for WD (Weight Distributing) and WC (Weight Carrying) ratings. Generally, tongue weight is 10 percent of the trailer. WDH rating varies.

Class I-Light-duty: 2,000#s maximum trailer weight - 200# tongue weight and 300#s with weight distributing hitch.

Class II-Medium Duty: 3,500#'s maximum trailer weight - 300# tongue weight and 500#s with weight distributing hitch.

Class III-Heavy-duty: 5,000#s maximum trailer weight - 7,500#s trailer weight with a weight distributing hitch, 300 – 500# tongue weight. Up to 750# tongue weight with weight distributing hitch.

Class IV-Extra-Heavy-Duty: 10,000 to 12,000#s and above maximum trailer weight depending on the manufacturer - 1,000# tongue weight with a weight distributing hitch.

Class V-Receiver hitch can be over 12,000#s. Class V doesn't exist yet by SAE standards. Ford started calling their heavy-duty receiver hitch Class V for the 2.5-inch shank for heavier trailers. The rest of the heavy-duty truck manufacturers joined in as well, as did most of the hitch manufacturers. As of publication, SAE hasn't finished their static and dynamic testing for an official Class V.

Caution: Always read the label on the hitch including factory-equipped receivers. Some hitches are rated for their maximum capacity only if you use a Weight Distribution Hitch. The side label on most receiver hitches will have a tongue weight and trailer weight rating of WD (Weight Distributing) and WC (Weight Carrying). WD is the capacity for weight distributing, WC is weight carrying as a drawbar with all the trailer tongue weight on the hitch.

TRUCK CLASSIFICATIONS

Class	Gross Vehicle Weight Rating Range	Examples
Class 1	GVWR 0 – 6,000 pounds	Frontier, Tacoma, Colorado, Canyon
Class 2	GVWR 6,001 – 10,000 pounds (subdivided into 2 classes, Class 2A & 2B, see below)	See class 2A & 2B below
Class 2A	GVWR 6,001 – 8,500 pounds	Ford F-150, Dodge Ram 1500, Chevrolet Silverado 1500, Nissan Titan
Class 2B	GVWR 8,501 – 10,000 pounds	Nissan Titan XD, Chevrolet Silverado 2500, Dodge Ram 2500, Ford F-250
Class 3	GVWR 10,001 – 14,000 pounds	Dodge Ram 3500, Chevrolet Silverado 3500, Ford F-350, Ford F-450 pickup
Class 4	GVWR 14,001 – 16,000 pounds	Dodge Ram 4500, Ford F-450 (chassis cab)
Class 5	GVWR 16,001 – 19,500 pounds	Dodge Ram 5500, Ford F-550, F-450 (chassis cab)
Class 6	GVWR 19,501 – 26,000 pounds	Ford F-650
Class 7	GVWR 26,001 – 33,000 pounds	Ford F-750
Class 8	GVWR over 33,000 pounds	Tractor Trailer

Trailer brakes and cab controls are needed on trailers weighing over 3,000 pounds. Surge brakes used commonly on boats will not have a manual control in the cab, but rely on the movement of the tow vehicle to activate the trailer brakes.

Bonus: Surviving and Saving Fuel. Low prices can't last forever.

Different trailer configurations can result in different MPG for your truck

As far as efficiency is concerned, 2,000 RPM is the sweet spot for most gas and diesel engines. This RPM generally translates to running at around 65 MPH. In my test of a conventional (bumper pull) 2-horse aluminum trailer compared to a gooseneck 3-horse steel trailer, the gooseneck got 3 MPG better fuel mileage, both trailers weighing about the same. The gooseneck trailer, with coupler in the truck bed, benefited from the air going over the truck cab and reaching to the gooseneck roof where the bumper pull trailer caught the air coming off the back of the truck's tailgate with more force. Anything that blocks air will increase drag and lower your MPG. I think the difference is less on larger, heavier trailers, as moving a larger mass will only get so efficient. Larger trailer wheel bearings and oil bath hubs basically roll easier. Not enough to warrant switching, but something to look at before you buy your next trailer. Which is the point: many accessories for your truck, such as larger exhaust, air intake, and power programmers, can increase your fuel mileage. But since accessories aren't free, how long will it take to pay them off with just the fuel savings? Adding a second fuel tank can get you past the states with higher fuel prices or allow you to buy more fuel when you do find a deal.

Let's look at what we can do for free: fewer trips, trailer pooling, vacations closer to home, and just slowing down when towing a trailer is a good start. Planning trips with a navigation system that takes construction and traffic into account and looking for the cheapest fuel on your trip routes are the best practices.

1. What is the single most important thing a person can do to help maximize fuel mileage? Slowing down. The faster you go, the more wind resistance you are subjected to. Fuel consumption increases dramatically above 60 mph, and it's just horrible above 75 mph. As much as we hate to drive 55, that is an ideal speed for better fuel economy. Air resistance becomes a factor above 50 mph. If your truck has an onboard fuel economy gauge, you can reset it at each speed and see an estimate of what your truck gets. In Colorado, our Interstate speed limit is 75 mph. My test showed 9 MPG at 70 mph, and about 12.2 MPG at 60 mph. That is a big difference!

2. If you use a slide-in truck camper towing a bumper pull trailer, the lighter "popup" campers are lower than big hard-sided ones and are thus more aerodynamic. The key to better fuel economy is less drag.

3. Using a tonneau cover on your truck with a bumper pull trailer will help it tow easier for better MPG. According to GM, it improves mileage by 6 percent.

4. Tailgate up. It's been proven to be better for MPG than down or off with a conventional tow trailer. Whether it helps with a goose-neck trailer is up for debate.

5. Keeping your truck healthy for better economy. I am a fan of synthetic oil. It flows easier and handles heat better than conventional oil. Synthetic oil in your truck's engine and axles has less friction, allowing engine and axles to take a little less power. Each year, more truck manufacturers switch to synthetic oil for axles, transmissions, and engines for fuel savings and longer life.

6. Keeping the proper air pressure in your truck and trailer helps your tires roll easier. Correct tire pressure helps tire life as well as improves fuel mileage. There are accessories that monitor your truck and trailer tire pressure from your cab. Some fuel savings come from balanced tires. The majority of trailer tires aren't balanced. Nitrogen is becoming more popular in tires, as it keeps them cooler, doesn't leak as fast, and keeps water/moisture out of the tires.

7. Good service and regular maintenance on your truck. A clean air filter and clean fuel filter help your engine work less. Waxing your truck and trailer can improve MPG. Speaking of clean, clean your truck cab and bed out. Extra weight costs fuel.

For automatic transmissions, cooling is a big deal for towing. Most modern trucks come with an automatic transmission temperature gauge on the dash, so you can keep an eye on above normal temperatures. You don't want to run over 300 degrees for too long. You can have an aftermarket external transmission cooler added. This looks somewhat like a small radiator and is in front of your main engine coolant radiator, along with a small cooler coil for your power steering and another small radiator-looking cooling core for the A/C. You can tell if one of the smaller cooling cores is for your transmission by tracking the rubber hoses to see if they go to the automatic transmission.

TOP 3 MPG TRUCKS

MOST FUEL-EFFICIENT TRUCKS FOR THE DAILY GRIND

What are the most efficient trucks in the land? The answer to this is a bit more complicated than simply looking up the government Environmental Protection Agency (EPA) ratings. As you already know, trucks with GVWR of over 8,500 pounds are not rated by the EPA. Even for those light-duty and midsize trucks that have government ratings, the way each truck is equipped can greatly affect its MPGs. The EPA does not provide MPG estimates for trucks with trailers, and real-world conditions can have a significant effect on the economy you get at the pump.

What is there to do but test various classes of pickup trucks on our 100-mile highway loop? OK, let's go! Let's get the real-world data. Please refer to Chapter 2 for a detailed description of "The Daily Grind" MPG testing procedure.

2016 Chevrolet Silverado 3500 HD Dually

Before we get to the 2016 finalists, let's discuss the factors that affect vehicle efficiency.

1) Vehicle Weight: straightforward physics says that an object of greater mass has a higher resistance to acceleration or directional changes. In other words: the lighter the vehicle, the easier it can accelerate and less energy/fuel is used to move it.

2) Vehicle Aerodynamics: once the vehicle is in motion, aerodynamics become more important as the speed increases. Lower co-efficient of drag improves fuel efficiency at speed.

3) Engine/Motor: a more advanced and efficient engine is an obvious benefit to fuel economy.

4) Transmission: a transmission that has lower energy losses due to friction, and gears that are best matched to an engine's power and differential gear ratio, is a more efficient setup.

5) Tires: this is precisely where the rubber meets the road. A harder compound tire with closely knit tread pattern will provide lower rolling resistance and higher efficiency.

Pickup trucks are challenged in terms of weight and aerodynamics. Trucks tend to have heavier frames, axles, and suspensions to carry and tow heavy weight. Their boxy designs look tough, but are not terribly aerodynamic. Many trucks are fitted with off-road biased tires with large tread spacing and "knobbies." Naturally, engines and transmissions are consistently being improved for more power and efficiency. There are many challenges to making a pickup truck efficient, but all manufacturers continue to push the boundaries of possibility.

CAFE Standards

Government plays a big role in the ongoing fight for fuel economy. CAFE standards and regulations are basically fleet MPG goals that each manufacturer must meet. These standards are enforced by the National Highway Traffic Safety Administration (NHTSA). These goals apply to the entire volume of vehicles each manufacturer sells in a given year. Small and large light trucks have their own CAFE standards that are more lenient than those for passenger cars.

There are several ways that manufacturers can meet the overall fleet CAFE standards. They can use their fuel-efficient passenger cars to offset the thirsty trucks. For example, Toyota sells many Prius hybrids that get a combined 52 MPG. This helps to offset the Tundra pickups that get an EPA combined rating of 15 MPG. This is called credit transferring or trading. Manufacturers can also sell credits to other manufacturers. **(CAFE - http://www.nhtsa.gov/fuel-economy)**

TOP LIST

Here are the Top 3 most fuel-efficient pickup trucks for the 2016 model year. These were picked from the three truck classes: mid-size, half-ton, and heavy. All trucks towed the identical 5,600 pound trailer. No matter if you are reading this in 2016, 2017, or 2020, technologies and design methods that are discussed here are applicable to trucks and vehicles in general for years to come.

3.
2016 GMC Sierra 1500 6.2L V8 8-Speed

General Motors introduced the EcoTec3 generation of engines for the 2014 model year. These included the 4.3-liter V6, 5.3-liter V8, and the 6.2-liter V8. EcoTec3 is a cryptic marketing name for combining the most-advanced internal combustion technologies of that era into an engine family. EcoTec3 engines include: an aluminum engine block with cast-iron cylinder liners, high compression combustion chambers, direct injection, cylinder deactivation, and continuously variable valve timing. All this mumbo jumbo means that the Chevrolet and GMC pickup trucks received the best engines of the time, not some leftover designs they picked up from a passenger car drawing board. These engines required millions of hours of computer simulation and countless test miles.

6.2L V8 & 8-speed Automatic	420 hp at 5,600 RPM / 460 pound-foot at 4,100 RPM
Rear axle ratio	3.42
Efficiency party trick?	V8 to V4 cylinder deactivation

At the heart of this 2016 GMC Sierra is a 6.2-liter EcoTec3 V8. This is the largest displacement and highest output engine in the light-duty half-ton segment. Power output is tuned for truck duty, and it kicks out 420 HP and 460 pound-foot. Full horsepower is reached at 5,600 RPM. The maximum torque is reached at a somewhat high (for a pickup truck) 4,100 RPM, but there is so much of it throughout the rev range that it will break loose the large rear tires with any semi-aggressive throttle input (even with traction control on). An 8-speed automatic transmission sends the power to the wheels. This 8L90 Hydra-Matic transmission became available in higher-end trim levels of the Chevy Silverado and GMC Sierra in 2015 and 2016 model years. The additional gears in this transmission help improve off-the-line acceleration and cruising efficiency.

This big V8 engine is very clever. It attempts to achieve two conflicting goals: high power output and high fuel-efficiency. We can verify that it succeeded on both counts by performing 0-60 MPH and highway MPG tests. One of the enablers of good fuel economy is the engine's ability to switch between V8 and V4 modes. The switch from eight to four cylinder is imperceptible, but there is a green V4 icon in the gauge cluster that lets you know that you are saving fuel. You cannot "lock" the truck in V4 mode. The truck tries to anticipate your need for full power and is eager to go to V8 mode at the slightest touch of the throttle.

GM has addressed the aerodynamics by redesigning the front-end, the door openings and seals, and by adding a deep front chin spoiler. The spoiler effectively lowers the truck to help with air flow.

Still, we put every truck through the tough real-world demand of the "Daily Grind" test. Fuel economy of each truck is measured after precisely 98 miles of cruising down the highway at 70 MPH with a tall dual-axle livestock trailer that is loaded to 5,600 pounds.

The 2016 GMC Sierra crew cab 4x2 model with the 6.2-liter V8, 8-speed automatic transmission and a 3.42 rear-end gear ratio registered an impressive 10.7 MPG according to the fuel pump. The truck is EPA-rated at 15 MPG city, 21 MPG highway, and 17 MPG combined. This is good enough for third place, but there is a slight blemish on this good result. GM recommends a more costly premium fuel for the 6.2-liter V8 engine. And we used 91 octane, the highest octane premium fuel available in Colorado.

2.

2016 Nissan Titan XD 5.0L Turbo-Diesel V8

We tested every class of truck using the same trailer, weight, and procedure for 2016. The all-new 2016 Nissan Titan XD came in second with an impressive performance on the "Daily Grind" highway MPG test.

What is the Titan XD? It's a new offering from Nissan that is meant to fill the void between the half-ton and three-quarter ton heavy-duty trucks. In other words, the idea for the Titan XD is to offer payload and towing capabilities that are superior to a half-ton truck without the harsher ride and handling characteristics of a heavy-duty truck. The resulting Titan XD with the all-new 5.0-liter Cummins turbo-diesel engine is a truck with a heavy-duty frame that has better towing and hauling stability than a half-ton truck without the harsh and bouncy ride quality characteristic of most heavy-duty trucks.

5.0L V8 & 6-speed Automatic transmission	310 hp at 3,200 RPM, 555 pound-foot at 1,600 RPM
Rear axle ratio	3.92
Efficiency party trick?	Lots of turbo-diesel torque

The truck is using a newly designed 5.0-liter Cummins V8 that is equipped with a single turbocharger for the final power rating of 310 horsepower at 3,200 RPM and 555 pound-foot of torque at 1,600 RPM. The torque rating fits a void between the 460 pound-foot of torque in a light-duty truck and 765 pound-foot of torque in a heavy-duty. This is an all-new engine that Cummins has been working on for years. A commercial version of this engine is also being used in medium-duty delivery vans and RV chassis. The Titan XD engine is paired to a 6-speed automatic transmission built by Aisin. This transmission, in slightly different tune, is also used in the Ram 3500 high-output Inline-6 Cummins turbo-diesel trucks.

Nissan's approach to getting good fuel economy is to use a turbo-diesel engine and an automatic transmission made by two reputable companies. Simply put, diesel engines are ideal for hauling heavy weight down the highway. They develop their maximum torque low in the RPM range and can tackle slight inclines without straining or the need to downshift into a lower gear.

The 2016 Nissan Titan XD crew cab 4x4 with the PRO-4X package and 3.916 rear-end gear ratio bested the GMC Sierra 6.2-liter by a noteworthy margin. The Titan XD registered 11.1 MPG at the pump after the 98-mile loop with the 5,600 pounds trailer. This was made even more impressive by the fact that it was riding on off-road biased General Grabber tires. The GVWR of the Titan XD exceeds 8,500 pounds. As such, the EPA does not provide a fuel economy rating for it.

Nonetheless, the truck was solid, stable, comfortable, and quiet during our highway run. Good job to Nissan for making a very confident towing truck.

1.

2016 GMC Canyon 2.8L I4 Turbo-Diesel

Should it come as any surprise that the 2016 champion of highway towing fuel efficiency is a midsize pickup truck with a 2.8-liter turbo-diesel inline-4 engine? Combining a smaller truck with a relatively small turbo-diesel engine is a recipe for one efficient pickup.

2.8L I4 & 6-speed Automatic transmission	189 hp at 3,400 RPM, 369 pound-foot at 2,000 RPM
Rear axle ratio	3.42
Efficiency party trick?	Small displacement and diesel torque

The motor produces 181 horsepower at 3,400 RPM and 369 pound-foot of torque at 2,000 RPM. GMC Canyon shares it with the Chevrolet Colorado. The 6-speed automatic transmission sends the power to the wheels. The engine is branded as a Duramax, although it does not have much in common with the big 6.6-liter Duramax turbo-diesel V8 in the heavy-duty trucks from GM.

The "baby" Duramax in this 2016 Canyon is the first usage of a turbo-diesel in a midsize pickup truck that is sold in the United States in nearly three decades. None of the competitors offer a diesel engine option in their trucks. Will the Nissan Frontier offer a Cummins turbo-diesel in 2017 or 2018? Will Ford bring the next

Ranger with a diesel? Will Toyota finally change their mind and start installing diesels in the Tacoma?

The little diesel in the Canyon behaves in a typical way. It uses the low-end torque for a good jump off the line, but when the truck goes beyond 40 MPH, the acceleration slows down. It cruises at highway speeds quietly and with minimal effort. It rarely needs to downshift, and it did not downshift many times pulling a 5,600 pound trailer at 70 MPH.

This GMC Canyon crew cab 4x4 SLT model with the 3.42 rear-end gear ratio is EPA rated at 20 MPG in the city, 29 MPG on the highway, and 23 MPG combined. It registered a commanding 12.3 MPG at the pump after the 98-mile highway towing test. It is a significant lead over the 11.1 MPG from the 2016 Nissan Titan XD Diesel and 10.7 MPG from the 2016 GMC Sierra 1500 6.2L V8.

What about real-world highway fuel economy for trucks with no trailer? There are two trucks that stood out above all others on our 98-mile highway loop. They are the 2016 Ram 1500 EcoDiesel HFE and the aforementioned 2016 GMC Canyon Diesel.

2016 Ram 1500 EcoDiesel HFE

What does the EcoDiesel HFE stand for? In Ram speak, it stands for High Fuel-Efficiency. The EcoDiesel is a 3.0-li-ter V6 turbo-diesel engine that makes 240 horsepower at 3,600 RPM and 420 pound-foot of torque at 2,000 RPM. It's paired with an 8-speed automatic transmission (designation ZF Torqueflite 8HP70). This is already an efficient drivetrain combination, but the HFE model takes it further with a tonneau cover and long running boards for improved aerodynamics on this low-slung 2WD truck. It's rated at 29 MPG on the highway by the EPA. Our real-world result was a solid 28.8 MPG. This is the best result in a full-size pickup truck that we have registered thus far.

2016 GMC Canyon Diesel

Yep, the "baby Duramax" makes a second appearance in this Chapter, and there is a very good reason to this. Just like the EcoDiesel HFE, it's also EPA rated at 29 MPG on the highway. It crushed the EPA rating when it got 31.3 MPG at the pump after the 98-mile loop.

MR. TRUCK

6

USED TRUCK
JUDGING 101

COMPARING TRUCKS

Now for the dark side. Used truck salespeople are the lions in the grass waiting for the gazelle or antelope to wander close. I've seen used sales folk throw customer keys on top of the store roof so they couldn't leave without making a deal. I've seen salespeople put the agreed price on a sales order with another sales order on top of it with a higher price to see if they got caught. And if they did, then they'd pull up the bottom one and act innocent because the higher price was for "another customer on another truck." I've seen a "buy here, pay here" bad credit store buy an envelope of titles from cars that were crushed and use them as down payments for people without money down. But that was at a good dealership...

Get Hard is a movie starring Will Ferrell about a rich guy hiring a poser to toughen him up for prison. That's what you need before going shopping for a used truck. Get that mean look that would scare John Wayne, do your research, and take control. Used trucks don't have an invoice, most trades are taken in at thousands below what the KBB blue book or NADA yellow book said the truck was worth, and what trucks like it were selling for at auctions around the country. Most of the trucks at a used lot come from dealer auctions. If it doesn't sell on their lot, thirty days later, back to the auction it goes. Lemons, buybacks, flood damage, all the junk makes it to the auction. Very low mileage trucks might have spent most of their lives in the shop with chronic repairs. But with millions of used trucks out there, you can find good used trucks. I know it sounds old school, but going late on a Saturday night on the last day of the month can still give you leverage at negotiating.

I buy and sell vehicles on Craigslist for my collection. Sometimes there's a deal, sometimes it's a scam. But I've seen good trucks there with real phone numbers instead of text messages for someone who's selling the truck for their girlfriend, and the game goes on and on. It's all about patience and research. But judging a used truck for its condition is the same no matter what. Negotiating price, again, is patience, but you have to add some gangster attitude. One-owner trucks that pulled light trailers and were garaged their whole life would be ideal. Those ads might be on Craigslist, or in the local paper, or even at garage sales in high-end neighborhoods.

How much off-road use does this truck have (below)? Trucks with off-road packages are fun, but like a Corvette or Mustang GT, people buy them to run them hard. Some trucks become rock climbers on weekends.

2016 Toyota Tacoma 4x4 TRD Off-Road

Judging your best-used truck: This is a job that requires work. You are in charge. You're the customer. Find out the facts about the trucks that are important to you. When I sold trucks on a Saturday (big sale day), the service center would be closed. If I wanted to show a used truck where the customer wasn't sure how good my truck was, I drove the truck into the empty service center. Then I pulled out two creepers, and the customer and I would then slide under the truck and look for oil leaks and old mud caked in the frame from extreme off-road use. Some used vehicles tour auctions from around the country and come from the last hurricane, tornado, or flood area. It's a smart thing to wonder about a truck that has sand and mud stuck to the starter, and where do you suppose the seaweed wrapped around the U-joint came from? When you go to a used car lot, nothing stops you from bringing a creeper. Now get your creeper, flashlight, notepad, and oil rag to have some fun on test drives.

The Truck Nuts on the next page are judging a used truck. Don't forget to crawl under the used truck you're looking at. You can have your mechanic inspect it, but feel free to whip out your creeper and get under the truck where a lot of rust, oil leaks, and caked-on dirt will give you clues to the truck's previous life. When I was an auto broker with the AAA Auto Club, some of the members we helped buy vehicles for would bring along a mobile mechanic to check out a used vehicle. That's a very good idea; or take the used truck that you've narrowed down to a trusted mechanic. The mechanic will have a checklist to know if the truck's drivetrain is sound along with engines, computers, and sensors. If you are an AAA member, they have a great service to certify mechanics that you can trust.

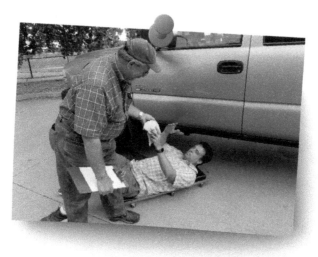

I worked in dealerships for ten years after leaving the farm. I saw people work so hard to get the right price on their truck just to give it all back by buying an overinflated, bogus warranty. The right warranty on your pickup can save you a lot of money. But don't fall for the high-pressure tactics to buy a warranty at the same time you buy your truck. You did your research on which truck you need, why would you buy a warranty from a stranger without a comparison and money-back guarantee?

Your new, used truck is an important decision that you don't make often. This makes research a big part of your success. Your first research will be looking at reviews on the web. Then, impartial forums to see what truck owners are saying about their last choice. Truck reviews on www.TFLtruck.com and www.MrTruck.com are good sources for truck reviews. Owner forums will give you truck owner opinions. For RV trailer towing trucks, www.RV.net is good, for trucks towing horse trailers, look at www.HorseTrailerWorld. com under the forum "trailer talk." There are so many things to look for on a previously-owned truck. You've heard of looking at the hinges for over-spray if it's had a paint job. Bring a magnet in your pocket to find excessive body putty. You can take the VIN (vehicle identification number) of the truck to that truck's manufacturer service center to look up recalls and the service record while under warranty.

Is this the truck you're looking at in the dealership this week? Guess where it was last weekend?

Next, take a good look at the seats and under the seat to see the springs. Note the thickness of the fabric and the stitching. Some fabric is sewn and glued to the foam and some is just stitched. The dealer is going to try to hide things, so look under the carpet mats, behind the rear seat. Look at the rubber gaskets around the doors and windows and excessive wear where you get in and out of a truck. Double check the mileage. Get a feel for how the inside controls are, can you reach them without being distracted? It's easier to get statistics on engines and drive-trains than the overall quality of a truck. Some years are better than others, and some plants are better than others. Competition has improved dramatically in the last few years, which is the driving force for quality. In Chapter 3, we talked about brand loyalty. I may not be able to convince you to switch truck brands. I wouldn't mess with your religion. But this is important on a used truck: the condition, past use, mechanical shape, and miles can be more important than the brand. Keep an open mind. Avoid the trucks that look like a work-aholic. Do you know what the used truck you're considering was doing in its previous life? Drag racing, towing ships, fording rivers maybe, or towing the space shuttle.

Some dealers will let you take the truck home. Then, you can take your time looking under and all over it. This would be a good time to tow your trailer with it. The size of the truck you need depends of course on your needs. Half-tons and light-duty three-quarter tons are for light-duty work, loaded part-time. Heavy-duty three-quarter tons, one-tons and above are designed to be loaded all of the time. They have twice as many tapered bearings that distribute weight in the rear axle housing. It's called a full-floating axle, similar to semi-truck eighteen-wheelers.

Full Floating Axle

Half-ton pickups have a semi-floating axle similar to a car, with just two bearings. With the heavy-duty three-quarter ton, one-ton trucks and larger, the rear axle housing will actually stick out past the wheel and have an additional eight bolts on the end of the hub holding the axle into the wheel hub with the axle "floating" between the wheel hub and differential. Rolls Royce invented the "full-floating" axle before WWII. Take a large screwdriver or pry bar to pop off the rear hubcap if you are looking at three-quarter tons and larger.

You will need to see if the truck has a full floating axle that sticks out on the Heavy Duties. GM, Dodge and Ford had some years in the eighties with light-duty three-quarter tons, (F250, 2500) which are half-tons with more wheel studs and higher rear spring ratings, but not full-floating axles. Ford did it again with a 7 wheel bolt F250 in 1997. This could happen again.

In Chapter 4 there is a truck classification chart. Generally, a half-ton truck is a Ford F150, Ram 1500, GM 1500, Toyota Tundra, or Nissan Titan. A three-quarter ton is a Ford F250, Ram 2500, or GM 2500. One-ton is a Ford F350, Ram 3500 and GM 3500.

The new in-between Nissan Titan XD has a semi-floating axle. The "semi-floating axle" has the wheel studs attached to it, carrying the truck's weight directly on the axle shaft and bearings. It's different on a "full-floating axle," where the axle shafts only provide power to the wheel hub from the differential. The wheel hub is attached to the axle housing with two tapered bearings on each side. On a full floating axle you can pull the axle out and the wheels are steel attached to differential axle tubes. This puts the load carrying capacity on the axle housing, not on the axle shaft as with a semi-floating axle.

Heavy-duty three-quarter tons, one-tons and larger will have heavier springs, shocks and in some cases thicker, stronger frames. In recent years pickup truck manufacturers have designed a different look between the half-ton and three-quarter ton. The majority of the time, if you compare a half-ton to a three-quarter ton pickup with the same gas engine option, the price is very close. And the three-quarter tons will usually have more rear axle ratio and tow package options. Because of the value of a three-quarter ton versus the price of a half-ton, I usually recommend a heavy-duty three-quarter ton. But keep in mind, because of a slight weight difference and the higher axle ratio in a half-ton pickup, a half-ton can have better gas mileage and a better ride. The EPA doesn't test fuel mileage on three-quarter ton trucks if they are over 8,500 pounds GVWR, so you won't find a fuel mileage rating on three-quarter ton and higher trucks.

The Used Truck Judging List

1. Shake, rattle, and roll. Does the truck vibrate excessively at idle? Does it shimmy at highway speeds? Is it needing just tire balancing or bigger parts? Oil slicks? I thought the oil went INSIDE the engine! Is oil dripping from the transmission, engine, differential, power steering, transfer case, etc.? Are those same components wet with oil? In my younger years, we expected trucks to use and leak oil. Newer trucks do none of that. Anything else leaking, gas, antifreeze, brake fluid? Any smoke from the exhaust? Is it black, blue, or white? Generally, black smoke is from over-fueling a diesel for power as in aftermarket tuners, blue can mean oil ring wear with blow by and usually an engine using oil, and white smoke is usually steam, as in water leaking from head gaskets. Any holes in the bed? Are they from toolboxes or a trailer hitch? See #5.

2. Get the TSB (Technical Service Bulletin) available at http://
www.nhtsa.gov/cars/problems/trd/#TECHNICAL on the truck
you're examining. It will show the recalls and modifications sent
to dealer service departments to fix known problems. Not all of it
may pertain to your truck. There are also crash tests and the EPA
mileage on trucks 8,500 GVWR and lower.

3. Run a CarFax report on the truck. Some dealers are doing this
now for you; this will show repairs and collisions. You'll want to
know if the truck has a clean title or salvage title. A salvage title is
for a truck that was rebuilt from other trucks, like Frankenstein.
It's hard to finance a salvage title. Also take the VIN (Vehicle Identification Number) usually on the left base of the windshield) to
a dealer for the brand of truck you are considering and have the
service department check the history with the brand's national da-
tabase. Then you will know if there are any open recalls or known
problems. And they can tell you if there is any remaining factory
warranty. Don't assume if the truck has less than 36,000 miles
that there is warranty left. Some factory buy-back lemons go to
auction and back to a car lot with low miles and without warranty.

4. Find out the rear axle ratio. We discussed the formula for axle
ratio in the last Chapter. Most trucks will have the axle code in
the driver door frame or in the inside of the glove box door. There
is usually a tag on one of the rear differential bolts with the ratio
info on it (another reason for bringing your own creeper). When in
doubt, get the service department to help you decode it.

5. Look under the surprisingly new bed liner to see what the bed
floor really looks like. A lot of the time, the new bed liner is to hide
the holes from the gooseneck hitch. Dealers quite often try to hide
evidence of any kind of hitches. I don't worry if a truck has a rear
receiver, especially if it was part of a factory tow package. But a
hole or holes in the bed where a fifth wheel or gooseneck ball was
attached, might be a truck to avoid unless it's exceptional in every
other way. There is no way of knowing how big a trailer was pulled
with the truck. Most of the folks I know who pull trailers usually
pull one that is a little too heavy. If the truck pulled a trailer that
was thousands of pounds over capacity (like I would), it can strain
the drive train and necessitate premature transmission, clutch,
U-Joint and axle replacement.

6. If you're looking at an automatic transmission, be sure to look
for an external transmission cooler. No, I'm not talking about the
lines that go through the radiator unless it's a GM truck, but a sep-

arate cooler in front of the radiator. If you are sure the truck didn't pull a trailer in a previous life, then you can add an external tranny cooler if the rest of the truck checks out.

7. Don't forget to use dealer math on figuring out how old the truck is. Look at the build date month/year, which is on the sticker inside the driver's side door. Use this to more accurately determine the truck's age. Vehicles do a weird thing in the fall when the new model comes out. The used trucks all get a year older in September instead of January. Remember that because book value will go down on your used trade-in, so don't forget to remind your opponent that the truck they are trying to sell you lost some value, too. With 0 percent interest on new trucks, like last fall and this summer and fall, more trade-ins are flooding the used auto lots. Expect more selection and lower prices on trucks this fall. The price you get for your trade-in will certainly be lower. It works both ways-don't forget to remind the salesperson of that.

8. You've been told this for years, but it's still true: sell your trade yourself for the most money. And it's easier to know where you are in the deal. If you're in Colorado, your sales tax is figured on the difference between your trade and what you are buying, except on a lease. Forget to take your trade-in. Just working with the numbers on one truck, not a truck and a trade-in, clarifies what you are really paying. Dealers like to jack the price up on their truck and pretend to give you more than they really are for your trade. Then they can drop their price some and look good because they are giving you so much for your trade (not). Add sales tax on the truck you're buying to what you are getting for your trade or ask for your trade if you sell it yourself to see the whole picture.

9. If you look at a diesel, don't forget to call the brand service department with the VIN again. The gas engine and truck has a 36,000 mile or thirty-six-month factory warranty. The diesel by itself will have a five-year or 100,000-mile warranty from the factory. On a diesel, it's important to have the mechanic check the radiator fluid and maybe have it tested for metal and oil. And the other side, check the oil and see if there is any water in it. With diesels, it's important that the radiator fluid had a conditioner added at the right service interval. If the radiator fluid gets bad, it can pit the sleeves and water jacket, which is called cavitation.

10. If the VIN checks out and the service records show the truck is clean, look for any remaining factory warranty. What you find will be fixed, but if there are a lot of things wrong it will cost too much time. Check the gaskets around the driver's door, the threshold,

the carpet, and the pedals to see if the wear matches the miles on the odometer. Check the paint for over-spray by the door hinges, hood hinges, and where the fenders meet the liner. The fenders should match other body parts' alignment and gap. Try each gear, including reverse, with the brake on to see how fast it engages each gear and how much play (roll) it has. If it moves too much before you feel the axle move, you could have wear in the pinion gear or U-Joints. If you hear too much noise in the tranny when you engage, then there is another problem. Once again, if the truck has factory warranty, all these things can be fixed and you have peace of mind; I just don't want to see you with chronic problems. The mechanic can check how the tranny engages. And check the normal stuff, seeing what comes out of the exhaust: water, oil, or carbon monoxide. Check out the 4x4, shift on the fly, engage the button or dial, put in 4x4 high with the hubs in auto or lock and do the circle to see if it hops. This is what you want. Unless it's an all-wheel drive or full-time 4x4, it won't hop driving in a circle. Then stop the truck and put in 4x4 low and drive slower in a circle. And if a manual 4x4, do the same with the floor lever and the hubs engaged. Some 4x4 trucks have solid front hubs like a front wheel drive car. They are always on and you engage the transfer case with a lever or switch.

A used diesel not maintained properly and over-pulled beyond its factory weight ratings can be an expensive time bomb. Diesel mechanics charge more than gas engine mechanics per hour. Engines, radiators, alternators, starters, batteries, etc. all cost more for diesel engines. If a diesel truck wasn't serviced properly with the more expensive gas, filters, and cooling fluid additives, etc., and if the truck pulled trailers way beyond the GCWR limits, which is common, then buying a 100,000-mile diesel truck may cost you a fortune. Buy a used diesel truck with a pedigree from a one-owner, pulling moderate trailer weights and having service receipts is worth a premium.

Now trucks, since they have better resale value and generally last longer, can be priced even higher at one-year-old than new. I have seen that happen often. To see a significant difference, you need to go back 3 years in trucks. A common misconception is that a three-quarter ton truck costs more than a half-ton truck. It's true if the heavy-duty is a diesel. But if both trucks have gas engines, they will be very close in price. Consider your future needs–maybe a bigger trailer or camper.

Auto transmissions in diesels in the past were an expensive lesson. The problem wasn't so much the tranny, but diesels are hard on drive trains. An auto transmission multiplies the torque from the engine through the torque converter. It's easier to manage your speed in reverse with an auto tranny, even though in a 4x4 you can put the transfer case in low range to help a manual transmission slow down. With the modern trucks and hydraulic clutches, you can't use the free play left on the pedal to check wear, but you can judge if the pedal backs almost all the way out before engaging. The farther out the clutch comes, the more wear it has. The original factory warranty — if still in effect — will generally cover an automatic transmission repair, but rarely do warranties cover clutches.

The greatest weapon a salesperson has against you is your own emotions. Knowing about your excitement over a new-to-you truck, salespeople are trained to ask about and use your "Hot Buttons." Think of the truck as a chunk of metal and plastic, just like the salesperson does. Your opponent will use some logic to justify the emotional decisions they are pushing. Usually, you will always find another great deal, so don't get into a rush. Make an educated, logical, wise, and economical decision. You can get all excited on the way home in your new-to-you truck and keep your kids' college fund in your bank. I'm amazed how it's passed down for generations: the belief that a salesperson we just met is a truck expert. I've been in the auto business for ten years now, and have met very few salespeople who could give truthful, helpful answers to pickup truck questions. There is a place for sales and marketing, and both are needed professions. But it's not exactly fair when you buy a vehicle every four or five years and your "trusted salesperson" sells everyday! Good trucks can last a long time, and so can the wrong one. I've seen people hurt their credit rating by buying the wrong truck and then having to go back and trade in that wrong truck for a lot less than they just paid. Now they have the right truck, and their payment is $300 higher. It's always the nice people too! The tough truck buyers, like in everything else, get their invoice deal and move on.

It's hard to recommend which truck without knowing what you are going to use it for. In the big cities people use them as cars. When I first came to Denver, I was amazed to see five-year-old pickups with no scratches in the beds. My pickups didn't last the first day without a scratch. After you drop the first salt block and the first big round bale, the bed just doesn't look the same. It's your money, your time, and your fun! I've driven my share of daily driver trucks lasting over twenty-plus years or more. I've got a 1970 Chevy C10 now that I'm restoring and plan to use as my parts runner. And on Friday nights, we'll take it to the Sonic drive-in and tell wild lies about all the work I did on it.

I believe in long test drives and several of them. Always remember it's your money and you are in control.

Disclaimer: This report contains my experience, opinions, and research. Use this as a guide to make an intelligent choice on your own.

GAS
OR
DIESEL
ENGINE

MR. TRUCK

Diesel engines are a big part of judging used trucks for trailer-towing. We've touched on diesels throughout the book, especially Chapter 3 and Chapter 6. This Chapter tries to answer the final decision. The right diesel can dramatically out-pull a gas engine. Ever see a gas-powered semi-truck? Diesels will generally last longer and get better fuel economy. At the present time they have better resale value. It's easy to become addicted to the power of a diesel. Diesels have more torque at lower RPM's than gas engines. On fuel mileage, the diesel can at times double the mileage of a gas engine. But they cost from $8,000 to over $11,000 over a new gas engine/transmission combination. It generally takes 150,000 miles of fuel savings to pay for the extra cost of a diesel versus a gas engine. So if you keep a truck a long time, after 150,000 miles the rest is gravy. If you trade often and don't pull a trailer a lot, you should consider a gas engine. But if you keep them a long time, or pull trailers constantly, the cost of the diesel option will pay for itself in fuel savings. And you can drive in the fast lane with a trailer.

You know diesels are louder than gas engines depending on the year. Diesel explodes from compression and heat inside the combustion chamber of your engine, while gas ignites from your spark plug. You really don't notice this flying down the road. But if you live in town, you'll notice the guy down the street who starts his diesel at 4 a.m. and warms it up for an hour, and the people at the drive-up windows seem to notice you in an older diesel. If you buy a diesel with a manual transmission, it will require more skill to shift. The compression is twice that of a gas engine, which means you have to shift faster and time the RPM's a little closer for a smooth shift.

The Bright Side: Light-duty diesel trucks are changing with 2016 midsize trucks from GM, and Colorado and Canyon have a diesel engine that can get over 30 MPG on the highway in real-world testing. These have only one battery and a 4-cylinder engine, so oil changes will cost less. It's a 2.8L baby Duramax manufactured in Thailand as a world diesel.

Earlier in 2014, Ram introduced an Eco Diesel 3.0L V6 in the 1500 with an 8-speed automatic transmission rated at 29 MPG on the highway. With these two fuel mileage champs, a diesel option in midsize and ligh-duty trucks costing less than $5,000 could pay for itself from fuel savings closer to 50,000 miles.

These two trucks, or call it three trucks, can change the rules for diesel economics. Both are rated to tow trailers over 7,000 pounds giving impressive cost per mile numbers. Of course they are smaller engines, so towing in the mountains will not be in the fast lane.

The Down Side: Some heavy-duty diesels command a premium of over $11,000. If you keep them a long time, or pull trailers constantly, the cost of the diesel option will be minimized. In very cold conditions (-10 F°) you will need to plug in block heaters and be sure you are using blended fuel, #2 and #1. The ever popular "if you get diesel on your hands while filling your tank you will smell it for a few days" option. Oil changes will cost twice as much or more than gasoline-powered trucks, and in areas where you are required to have an emission test on trucks, the diesel costs more.

Diesels need the heat from glow plugs and/or manifold heaters to aid in warming up the cylinders for starting. Normally diesels run on #2 diesel. #2 has lubricating qualities (paraffin wax, that make it oily, smelly, and stays on your hands for a few days). #1 diesel is like kerosene or jet fuel and less oily. The lubricating properties in #2 are what gels when it gets extremely cold. This is why a blend of #2 and #1 50/50 is used in the winter by most service stations in states that get cold. If you go to a warm state (California, Arizona, Florida, etc.) in the winter and buy fuel there before coming home to a cold state, you may want to use a diesel additive. If you are in an unfamiliar place, buy your diesel at a truck stop. They should know what you need.

If you have never experienced gelling up a diesel in the winter, be happy. I have had this experience on my farm tractors. I had to use a hair dryer to liquefy the fuel in the injector pump and then "crack" the fuel lines to bleed the fuel through the pump and injectors. Most states don't get cold enough to plug in the block heater on your diesel. But if you are in colder areas and need to plug in your diesel, I like to use a timer you can buy from WalMart for $12 to $15. You only need to set the timer to turn on for a couple of hours before you're ready to use your truck.

In Colorado, you get four years of emission exemption when the truck is new, and after that you are required to be tested every two years in certain Front Range counties. Today, the break-in period on new engines is generally 500 miles for gas engines and 1,000 miles for diesel engines. During that time, you don't want to use your cruise control. You need to vary the RPM's so the valves and rings can seat properly through the whole RPM range. On a diesel it generally takes 5,000 miles to adjust itself. After that, diesels tend to start faster and the fuel mileage is set to be as good as it gets from the factory.

Diesel is safer to handle than gas in case of a fire. With the new turbo diesels, smoke is not the problem it used to be before turbos. Diesels need enormous amounts of air. Above 10,000 feet of elevation your turbo diesel loses about 4 percent power per 1,000 feet. Not many people drive that high. Newer diesels will cut back on power at 8,500 feet, so they don't over-fuel and smoke and plug up the diesel particulate filter. Since diesels rely on compression combustion, the engine components are built heavier than gas engines. Curiously, the diesel mechanic rate per hour is also higher than for gas engines.

Most of these diesel engines have a bleeder valve on or near your fuel filter to drain off water from the fuel; diesel engines are prone to condensation in the fuel tanks. If you pay close attention to servicing your fuel filter, air filter, oil, oil filter, and radiator at the right intervals, you should expect to join the 300,000-mile club with your diesel pickup truck.

Diesel fuel cost relative to gasoline varies seasonally and among the different states. Although, diesel tends to be more expensive than gas these days. Diesel has been a cheaper fuel for decades. Trains run on diesel and jets run on #1 diesel, as well as ships, semitrucks, farm tractors, and Abrams M1 tanks. Part of the problem is the EPA war on diesels. Emission controls on new diesel trucks rob power, create heat, and make us use Diesel Exhaust Fluid (urea). DEF and particulate filters are the latest scrubbing systems for clean diesel. Ram Cummins diesels didn't use DEF fluid until 2013 – Ford and GM starting using DEF in the 2011 model year.

DIESEL PARTICULATE FILTERS: A HOT SUBJECT

In January 2007, the new emission law went into effect for diesels. Of course, the new diesel engines designed for lower emissions cost more, have EGR coolers, throttles, use more expensive CJ4 low ash classification engine oil, and have a Diesel Particulate Filter. The DPF is where pollutants are trapped and burned off when it regenerates. With the new ultra-low sulfur diesels–Ford 6.7L, Dodge 6.7L and GM 6.6L LMM–all have a Diesel Particulate Filter. DPF can get to 1,100 F° when it's regenerating (burning up the NOx). If the DPF is almost full, it can take up to thirty minutes to burn out as you drive. If you remember when catalytic converters first came out, we had many wheat field and grass fires. Look at the tailpipe on these new diesels; some look like a propane weed burner, but are designed for cooling the exhaust where it leaves the truck.

As you run your diesel, sensors in the DPF measure the amount of particulate matter that is accumulating in the filter and send that data to the engine computer that controls the engine and after-treatment process. When DPF sensors tell the engine computer that the DPF is filling up, a self-cleaning process called regeneration will raise the temperature in the DPF by turning on an injector during the exhaust stroke to oxidize the particulate matter.

In some trucks you can smell the DPF regeneration and feel some power gain when finished. Under normal operating conditions, you don't need to do anything. If you do a lot of city driving or hours of idling, your engine may not be working hard enough to regenerate. This can cause warning lights to let you know that your truck needs highway time to clean the DPF. If you drive after the warning lights come on too long, the DPF gets too full, and you will lose power and damage the expensive filter. Read your owner's manual.

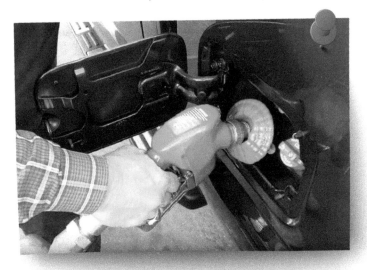

There are aftermarket engine programmers on the market now that will force the engine to regenerate when you want to, like before that 15-mile grade in Utah or the sled-pull at the county fair.

All the truck manufacturers, including semi-trucks, are going with urea (diesel exhaust fluid) to lower emissions. If your diesel truck runs low on DEF fluid, you'll get warnings, then the next warning will slow you down and then slow you down to a crawl. When you are running low on DEF and you may not make it to the next Walmart to buy more DEF fluid, don't shut off your truck. It usually should just take a restart to get to the next warning. But it's still better to carry a few extra gallons of DEF with you.

So many things like that – and the fact that diesels sell more new in the 4x4 extended or crew cab HD – makes finding a good used gas engine HD truck hard, thus holding resale value. So the range I see between a used diesel and a used gas truck isn't nearly the spread as when new. I like diesels, too, but it's like the 4x4 SUV thing: people buy them because they like them more than because of a need. And this goes for diesels, too.

Did you catch that? In heavy-duty, you'll find more used diesel trucks than gas-powered trucks. It's a case you could make either way and not be wrong. But I do like to bring up points contrary to the majority-thinking. With service costs, diesels are more expensive with filters for air, fuel, water, and 10 to 15 quarts versus 5 to 8 quarts for gas engines. And you know what a starter for a diesel costs, and the bigger alternator. I didn't want to bring up the noise because diesels are getting quieter.

I also think buying a used diesel is harder to do than a gas truck. If you don't know how the truck was serviced, how much the trailer weight was over the truck's capacity, etc., then a used diesel can be an expensive time bomb because of water jacket cavitation, oil consumption, pump failure, glow plug failure, etc.

I see city folks all the time buying diesel trucks to get groceries and use as a car; they never cycle the glow plugs, have no clue where to drain the water out of the fuel filter, don't know when to add the conditioner to the coolant, etc. And then the next person who gets the truck spends $10,000 on it the first year, with the warranty void because service wasn't done by the previous owner and the mechanic finds a pitted water jacket, scored cylinder walls, plugged fuel filters (didn't know it had two), etc. I'm starting to scare myself, so I better quit. This is a good topic for everyone's input, because it's not as clear-cut as it might seem.

The present HD diesels — GM, Dodge and Ford — get the power boost for the brakes from the power steering; it's a hydraulic boost instead of a vacuum boost. Recently, Ford has gone back to vacuum brake boosters on F250 diesels.

If you notice when you're in a tight spot sitting still and you try to turn the steering wheel while your foot is on the brake you will notice you can't steer much. The brake boost is robbing from the steering boost. When the engine dies for whatever reason, there is of course nothing turning the power steering pump, so you're down to manual steering and no brake boost. You still have hydraulic brakes but you have to push harder.

The power of a diesel is addicting, and that power is the biggest reason for buying a diesel. Diesel mechanics charge more than gas engine mechanics per hour, and engines, radiators, alternators, starters, 2-batteries, etc. all cost more.

So when I mention taking around 150,000 miles for a HD diesel engine to pay for itself with fuel savings, I'm calculating how long it takes to pay for the extra $8,000 to $11,000 for the diesel option and the extra cost of servicing. Since I can't predict accurately future resale value, I can't add that back in. Five years from now, we could have the EPA ban all new diesels, or hydrogen cell technology could make the hybrids take over the market. Or maybe a new president will make diesels (and a gun rack) mandatory for all government vehicles. Or maybe I should go back to decaf. I love diesels, too, but I also look at "the bigger picture." And I do value all opinions on diesel versus gas, but it usually ends up like the bumper-pull versus gooseneck, Ford versus GM versus Dodge, John Deere versus Massey Ferguson, Baptist versus Methodist, ...regular versus decaf.

Now we're getting analytical. My point is HD diesels don't save you dramatically over a gas engine as they once did. The underlying reason folks buy diesels is power.

The diesel side of the debate gets championed more than the gas side. I like to show more than one viewpoint. If you tow heavy trailers the majority of the time, the diesel makes sense as with over-the-road semi-trucks. But the majority of truck owners now use their trucks as a car and pull trailers less than 25 percent of its life.

Sometimes I get emails from folks telling me how shocked they were at their first oil change cost of $75 to $100 on a diesel. Back when our choices in the late eighties were the new Dodge Cummins diesel in 1989 or a just fuel-injected Ford 460 or GM 454, then diesels could get twice the fuel mileage of a gas engine.

Now we have gas engines that without a load can get 14-16 MPG versus a diesel's 17-21 MPG highway miles and loaded pulling a trailer at 8-11 versus a diesel at 14-16 MPG. Bottom line, not everyone who pulls a trailer would save money with the diesel option. My mission is showing the strengths of the minority view.

Yes indeed, diesels use very little fuel at idle allowing truckers to keep the truck running while they nap. And the carbon buildup in an idling gas engine is not conducive to long life. But the soot in a diesel engine will also build up harmfully if you shut off a diesel that has idled long.

In Europe, diesel passenger cars make up over 40 percent of the vehicles verses our less than 1 percent. In this country, VW has been offering an economical diesel car for several years now, but even they got caught breaking the EPA rules.

Europe is on the path that diesels are the future to economy and lowered air pollution, while politics in this country are toward alternative fuel and hydrogen cells. Actually, the engineers I interviewed think it's impossible to make the hydrogen cell save enough. VW has a major project underway with biodiesel, biomass called SunFuel, which will complete the circle with only CO_2 emissions going back to the plants to produce more biomass. I am not against diesels; I just don't think they fit every scenario, nor do I think everyone needs a dually to pull a trailer.

It's not my money and I ain't going to make your monthly payments. Borrow your neighbor's diesel and tow your trailer this weekend – you may get addicted, too.

ANDRE

8

TOP 5
HALF-TON
IKE
GAUNTLET

COMPARING TRUCKS

What is the best towing half-ton pickup in the land? The answer can only come from the extreme Ike Gauntlet towing test. We push the trucks near their limits in order to get to the truth. The trucks that perform well on this 8-mile stretch of the Rocky Mountain interstate with its 7 percent grade and 11,158 feet of elevation are the best towing pickup trucks. If they succeed in the extreme environment of the Ike Gauntlet, they will handle your next towing project with ease.

This is a very exciting time in the pickup truck industry. It's simply because truck makers are bringing so many solutions, advanced features, and a great variety of trucks to the market. Nowhere is it more evident than in the most popular segment – the half-ton (1500 series) trucks. This segment is home to the three most popular vehicles sold in the United States: the Ford F-150, Chevrolet Silverado 1500, and Ram 1500. They are still "The Big Three." Just consider the breadth of technologies these trucks are bringing forth.

The Ford F-150 is focused on lightweight aluminum construction and downsized turbocharged gasoline engines. Chevrolet and GMC are staying the more traditional course with the latest family of naturally aspirated V6 and V8 engines, and Ram is the only half-ton on the market with a small turbocharged diesel V6 engine.

Toyota and Nissan are not standing still. The Tundra is staying with the traditional V8s, while Nissan is mounting an assault with a two-pronged approach — a redesigned Titan XD and the half-ton Titan. More on this later.

What's in a name?

The 1500 series half-ton trucks are also known as light-duty pickups. These names come with historical significance, but do they still make any sense? The trucks I am talking about here are in what the United States defines as Class 2a. These are the trucks with a GVWR of 6,001 - 8,500 pounds. They are also called the 1500 series, or half-tons. Half-ton had real meaning two or three decades ago when these trucks were rated at about half-ton (or 1,000 pounds) of payload. These days, half-ton trucks, such as the F-150 with the heavy payload package, are rated up to 3,000 pounds of payload. Granted, this is a very specific configuration of an F-150. Still, this is a ton and a half of weight. Most pickups in this class are rated between 1,500-2,000 pounds of payload.

Should we still call them "half-tons"? Yes! The name has stuck, and people know what it refers to.

Ike Gauntlet for Half-Tons

You already have all the background on the Ike Gauntlet test from Chapter 2. The only thing left to explain is that we tow different weights for each class of pickup truck. In the case of half-ton light-duty trucks, it is a 9,000 pounds bumper-pull enclosed trailer.

Why 9,000 pounds? The goal is to push each truck to near its limit, and this trailer load is heavy enough to challenge any half-ton truck and it's light enough that every crew cab half-ton truck is able to safely tow it.

Safety is the most important thing for any test, and it is never more true than hauling and towing a heavy weight up and down the steepest interstate in the country. We carefully consider the GVWR and GCWR of every truck we test and make sure that the load (trailer and people) does not exceed these two ratings. Of course, there are many other limits we must also obey: maximum tow rating, maximum trailer tongue rating, maximum payload rating, and Gross Axle Weight Rating (GAWR) of each truck and trailer axle.

Does it seem like too much to think about while towing or hauling? Yes, but you can quickly simplify it. Chapter 4 goes into great detail about how to properly setup and load any trailer. Suffice to say that you should know the exact curb weight of your unloaded truck and the weight of your loaded trailer. Then it's a matter of a simple comparison.

GVWR ≥ Truck's Curb Weight + People + Cargo + Loaded Trailer's Tongue Weight

GCWR ≥ Truck's Curb Weight + People + Cargo + Loaded Trailer's Weight

If the GVWR and GCWR are not maxed out and there is a built-in safety margin, then all weight parameters will be within limits.

TOP LIST

Here are the Top 3 best towing half-ton pickup trucks for the 2016 model year. Each truck was scored on a 100 point scale that breaks down as such. There is a maximum 25 points for the downhill performance, maximum 25 points for the time up the mountain, maximum 25 points for the MPG up the mountain, and maximum 25 points for subjective reviewer opinion.

3.
2016 Chevrolet Silverado 6.2L V8
[Ike Score: 68]

What can be better than a big bad American V8 in a pickup truck? Few things are more American than that, but the 2016 Chevy Silverado with the 6.2-liter V8 lands in third place in this Ike Gauntlet competition. GM trucks and SUVs have grabbed many TFLtruck awards in the past. What gives? Let's look at the details.

6.2L V8 & 8-speed Automatic Transmission	420 hp at 5,600 RPM, 460 pound-foot at 4,100 RPM
Rear axle ratio	3.42
Towing party trick?	Lots of power

This Chevy is a traditional truck in the sense that it's powered by a large displacement 6.2-liter V8 that is the highest output engine in the half-ton truck segment. This motor produces 420 horsepower at 5,600 RPM and 460 pound-foot of torque at 4,100 RPM. It is paired to an 8-speed automatic transmission, which provides well-spaced gear ratios for efficiency and power delivery. So why did it take third place in this comparison? The answer lies with the downhill performance and leads to the subject of rear axle gear ratio. This particular truck is equipped with a relatively high rear-end ratio of 3.23. It means that for every one revolution of the drive shaft, the rear axle makes 3.23 revolutions. This is better for fuel efficiency, but it is not the best setup for best acceleration, total power delivery, or downhill performance. The transmission has a downhill grade shifting logic that takes the transmission to lower gears and uses the engine RPM to slow down the truck and the load it's carrying. The Silverado 1500 can be optionally equipped with 3.42 rear-end gears. It doesn't appear to be a big difference, but it's enough to affect how the engine, the transmission, and the rear axle are matched. The grade shifting can be a little more effective with a 3.42 rear-end.

The Chevy performed very well on the uphill. It had no issues with keeping the 60 MPH speed limit up the mountain, and it returned a respectable 4.0 MPG according to the trip computer. This efficiency looks incredibly low at first, but consider that the truck is running at wide open throttle up a 7 percent grade at high elevation with a 9,000 pound trailer. 4.0 MPG is a good result for a gasoline fed engine. Turbo-diesels tend to do better when loaded with the same weight. The Silverado recorded a time of 8 minutes, 7 seconds up the Ike Gauntlet, which is very close to the ideal time of 8 minutes up this 8-mile stretch of Rocky Mountain interstate.

The three reviewers: Mr. Truck (Kent Sundling), Nathan Adlen, and Andre Smirnov gave the truck a good subjective score of 18 out of 25.

At the end of the day, the Chevy Silverado with the big motor and the 8-speed automatic transmission tackled the extreme Ike Gauntlet towing test without much drama. A large displacement engine, latest engine and transmission technologies, a solid chassis, and a well-sorted suspension all amount to a very good tow rig that deserves to be in our Top 3 best towing light-duty trucks of 2016.

The 6.2L Chevy received 11 points on the downhill, 15 points on the uphill MPG, 24 points on uphill time, and an 18 point average on the subjective score.

2.
2016 Ram 1500 5.7L V8
[Ike Score: 69]

"That thing gotta HEMI?" Okay, this was an unfortunately catchy phrase from the Dodge Ram TV commercials in the early 2000s, but this 2016 Ram 1500 indeed has a 5.7-liter HEMI V8 engine. The engine has been tweaked and tuned to produce an impressive 395 horsepower at 5,600 RPM and 410 pound-foot of torque at 3,950 RPM. It offers variable valve timing and fuel-saving cylinder deactivation that Ram calls Multi Displacement System (MDS). It can run on four cylinders under light loads or at a steady cruising speed. The MDS operation is smooth and will generally go unnoticed by the driver. Unlike GM's cylinder deactivation system that has a clear V8 or V4 indicator in the middle of the gauge cluster, Ram's MDS does not have an indicator that is set by default.

5.7L V8 & 8-speed Automatic transmission	395 hp at 5,600 RPM, 410 pound-foot at 3,950 RPM
Rear axle ratio	3.92
Towing party trick?	It's still got a powerful HEMI

The HEMI-powered Ram 1500 can be configured with an 8-speed automatic transmission and a 3.92 rear axle gear ratio, as this test truck was. We always request a crew cab truck with 4x4 for our testing. Sometimes, we are not able to get the precise truck configuration that we requested and this Ram 1500 came to us as a 2WD. A two-wheel-drive Ram 1500 weighs about 180 pounds less than a comparably configured 4x4. We run all trucks in good weather and in 2WD mode, but we added 180 pounds of sand bags to the bed of this Ram to compensate for the lack of the 4WD components and to keep the test fair.

The HEMI engine is a great match to the 8-speed transmission and the 3.92 rear-end gear ratio. The truck pulled very strong up the hill. In fact, there were sections where Nathan had to let off the accelerator in order to maintain the speed limit. The Ram performed better than the Chevy on the downhill with nine brake applications (versus fourteen with the Chevy Silverado). Still, the truck's grade shifting logic could have done better.

The light-duty Ram uses a coil spring suspension with an optional air suspension. It makes for a comfortable ride, but the truck also squats more under heavy load than competitors that use leaf springs. We resolved the issue with a weight distributing hitch.

The two reviewers: Mr. Truck (Kent Sundling) and Nathan Adlen gave the truck a good subjective score of 18 out of 25. In fact, this is the same subjective score as that of the 6.2-liter Chevy Silverado.

In the end, the Ram 1500 HEMI was an outstanding performer at the Ike Gauntlet challenge. The truck was loaded to the maximum, yet the ride was comfortable and stable. It performed well in every category with the exception of relatively poor uphill fuel economy of 3.0 MPG. After the dust settled, it took the second place away from Chevy by just one point.

The 5.7L HEMI Ram 1500 received 16 points on the downhill, 10 points on the uphill MPG, 25 points on uphill time, and an 18 point average on the subjective score.

1.
2016 Ford F-150 5.0L V8
[Ike Score: 77]

How can the smallest and least powerful V8 among these three win this contest? Indeed, the 5.0-liter Coyote V8 powered F-150 is the half-ton class towing champion for the 2016 model year. It was a surprise for all of us at TFLtruck.com and MrTruck.com.

Ford has been laser-focused on the EcoBoost technology since the first turbocharged trucks started rolling off the production line in 2011. The company is chasing more power and higher efficiency by downsizing the engines, turbocharging them, and putting them into aluminum-bodied trucks. It has been very difficult for us to get our hands on a brand-new F-150 with the naturally aspirated "five-oh." We have tested several F-150s with either the 2.7-liter or the 3.5-liter EcoBoost twin-turbo V6s, and we know firsthand how powerful and quick these trucks can be. Turbos help bring back some of the power lost to the high elevation of our testing environments. So, what about this naturally aspirated V8?

5.0L V8 & 6-speed Automatic transmission	385 hp at 5,750 RPM, 387 pound-foot at 3,850 RPM
Rear axle ratio	3.55
Towing party trick?	Lots of low-end torque and good grade shifting

This motor makes 385 horsepower at 5,750 RPM and 387 pound-foot of torque at 3,850 RPM. It's mated to a 6-speed automatic transmission. No fancy 8-speeds here. It is the latest iteration of Ford's iconic 5.0L engine. It features an aluminum block with aluminum head and Twin Independent Variable Cam Timing (Ti-VCT). The engine is relatively lightweight, and the computer can tweak the valve timing to get the most out of the engine. The result is an engine that develops lots of torque low in the RPM range, and this naturally helps the truck to get going. The test truck was equipped with a 3.55 rear axle gear ratio.

What does all of this mean on the grueling Ike Gauntlet? This F-150 went up the hill with surprising speed when loaded to the max and clocked in a 8:12 time (that was just five seconds behind the Silverado with the 6.2-liter). The Ford also returned a relatively good 3.8 MPG on the way, according to the trip computer. This is super close to the 4.0 MPG in the Chevy. Where the Ford truly separated from the pack was with the downhill performance. It registered just three brake applications. The engine and the rear-end ratio worked beautifully in unison with the grade shifting algorithm of the transmission.

The two reviewers: MrTruck (Kent Sundling) and Roman Mica gave the truck a high subjective score of 19 out of 25. It is just one point higher than what the Chevy Silverado and Ram 1500 got, but it's higher nonetheless. Bottom line is, the Ford F-150 5.0L surprised us with its excellent power delivery in the difficult high altitude environment of the Rocky Mountains. It was the undisputed half-ton champion of the Ike Gauntlet challenge in 2016. The twin-turbo V6s are incredibly powerful, but perhaps, it's too early to retire the "good old" 5.0L V8. The 5.0L V8 Ford F-150 received 16 points on the downhill, 10 points on the uphill MPG, 25 points on uphill time, and an 18 point average on the subjective score.

Other Competition

What about the trucks from Toyota and Nissan? Where is the only turbo-diesel in the half-ton segment: the Ram 1500 EcoDiesel? These are great questions, and here are the answers.

2016 Toyota Tundra 5.7L V8
[Ike Score: 60]

The Tundra is in the game with a full lineup of half-ton trucks. We tested a crew cab truck with the TRD Pro and towing packages. This 5.7L V8 engine powered pickup represents the latest in off-road technologies that Toyota has to offer. It also has a towing package that checks all the right boxes: tow-haul transmission mode, integrated trailer brake controller, 4.30 rear axle gear ratio, transmission fluid temperature gauge, and higher capacity engine oil and transmission oil cooling systems. The engine has plenty of low-end grunt as it makes 381 horsepower at 5,600 RPM and 401 pound-foot of torque at 3,600 RPM. So, how come the Tundra did not make it into the Top 3 best towing half-ton pickups?

At the end of the day, it did not win in any of the four categories: downhill, uphill MPG, uphill time, and subjective score. The Tundra was fairly quick up the mountain at 8:18, but it was slower than the Top 3 trucks. It was in the mid-pack on downhill with eleven brake applications. It returned a low 2.9 MPG up the Ike Gauntlet and a low subjective score of 16. The Tundra got the job done, but it did not shine as bright as most of its competitors.

2016 Nissan Titan XD 5.0L V8
[Ike Score: 63]

What about the new truck from Nissan: the all-new Titan XD? This truck faces a difficult challenge of creating its own "XD" segment. The truck's capability is positioned between the traditional half-ton ligh-duty and three-quarter ton heavy-duty pickups. Nissan saw a void in the market for a truck that is comfortable and quiet, like a half-ton, but with a heavier frame and higher payload and towing capacity. The company launched the new Titan XD at the end of the 2015 calendar year, and you could only have one with a 5.0L Cummins turbo-diesel V8 in a crew cab configuration. About five months down the line, a redesigned 5.6L gasoline V8 joined the options list for the Titan XD. More cab configurations and a true light-duty Nissan Titan joined the lineup throughout the 2016 calendar year.

After getting the curb weight of the Titan XD 5.0L V8 PRO-4X, it became clear that we will be limited by the payload rating of the truck. The GVWR is 8,990 pounds, so we had to limit the trailer weight to 10,200 pounds. Considering that the truck was loaded near the maximum, and was towing a heavy-duty gooseneck trailer with twin dually axles, it returned a respectable result. It recorded nine brake applications on the way down, and completed the ascent in 8:44 at 3.9 MPGs. It could have done better on the downhill if the Cummins V8 was equipped with an exhaust brake.

In the end, it received a total Ike Gauntlet score of 63 points. We could not compare it apples-to-apples with any other truck, but the Cummins turbo-diesel pulled strong up the hill, and we look forward to testing Titan trucks in other configurations and engine options.

Ram 1500 3.0L EcoDiesel V6

The EcoDiesel V6 powered Ram 1500 is the only truck in the half-ton segment with a turbo-diesel option for the 2016 calendar year. There are rumors that Ford F-150 will offer a diesel for the 2018 model year, but the Ram has no competition in this space until then.

The EcoDiesel is king of half-ton truck fuel efficiency. It's EPA-rated at 29 MPG on the highway for the High Fuel Efficiency (HFE) model, which is a 2WD quad cab with a tonneau cover and full-length running boards. So how does it handle the grueling Ike Gauntlet?

For starters, the EcoDiesel version of the Ram 1500 is not rated for towing as high as a comparable Ram with the 5.7-liter HEMI. We tested a 4x2 Quad Cab Big Horn model with a maximum towing capacity of 7,950 pounds.

We loaded it with 7,850 pounds of trailer, people, and cargo. Once again, this is not an apples-to-apples comparison with the Top 3 trucks listed above. Those trucks were towing a different 9,000 pound trailer.

The EcoDiesel completed the job with stellar fuel economy of 6.1 MPG, according to the trip computer. Most trucks cannot do better than 4.0 MPG on the same stretch. On the flip side, it was also much slower than the rest, and the Ram clocked in a time of 9:03. This is nearly a minute slower than the others.

ANDRE

9

TOP 3
MIDSIZE
IKE
GAUNTLET

BEST TOWING MIDSIZE PICKUPS ON THE MOUNTAIN

What does it mean to be a "midsize" pickup truck? What are these pickups in the middle of? There was a time in America in the 1970s and 1980s when "mini" trucks were commonplace. They were Isuzu Pups, Chevy LUVs, Mazda, Toyota, and Datsun pickups among others. Consumers' taste began to change in favor of more interior space and higher levels of hauling and towing capability. Enter the midsize truck segment. These guys are bigger than the older mini trucks, but still smaller in stature than the half-tons. The midsize pickup truck market was red hot in the United States in 2016. Popularity of midsize trucks dwindled between 2011 and 2014, when the Chevy Colorado, Ford Ranger, GMC Canyon, and Honda Ridgeline all stopped production one after the other. The Nissan Frontier and class-leading Toyota Tacoma soldiered on. Now, most of the players are back in business and more are coming soon. The GM twins, Colorado and Canyon, are back in full force, as is the Honda Ridgeline. The next generation Ford Ranger will join the party in the 2018 calendar year. A Jeep Wrangler-based pickup truck and crossover-based Hyundai Santa Cruz are also in the cards. We might even see a crossover-based midsize truck from Ram.

By the time 2019 rolls around, the midsize pickup market segment may consist of at least eight name plates, which is up from just two entries in 2015. Who'da thunk it! There are plenty of trucks to choose from, but not all of them are meant for every task. Some are great at off-roading. Some are great at towing and hauling. Others are great daily-driver utility trucks. What is the best towing midsize pickup in the land? The answer can only come via the extreme Ike Gauntlet towing test. If you have already read Chapters 2 and 8, then you know precisely what the Ike Gauntlet is all about. In the case of midsize trucks, we use the same enclosed trailer loaded to 5,600 pounds. This is enough to max out most midsize pickups. This is truly an extreme test, and one that gets down to the truth. If a truck has any weakness related to towing, it will be revealed here.

Here are the Top 2 best towing half-ton pickup trucks for the 2016 model year. Each truck was scored on a 100 point scale breaking down as such: there is a maximum 25 points for the downhill performance, maximum 25 points for the time up the mountain, maximum 25 points for the MPG up the mountain, and maximum 25 points for subjective reviewer opinion.

2016 Toyota Tacoma 3.5L V6
[Ike Score: 58]

The Toyota Tacoma was fully redesigned for the 2016 model year. This is a big deal for many reasons. Truck redesigns do not happen very often, and it's been nearly ten years since Toyota introduced the previous generation of the Tacoma. Also, the Tacoma has been the midsize segment sales leader for many years. There were time periods when the Tacoma sold more units than all of its competitors combined. It used to command nearly 70 percent of the midsize pickup truck segment. Of course, this is all changing because of increasing competition from many automakers.

3.5L V6 & 6-speed Automatic transmission	278 hp at 6,000 RPM, 265 pound-foot at 4,600 RPM
Rear axle ratio	3.91
Towing party trick?	Lots more horsepower than before

The 2016 Tacoma has an all-new 3.5-liter V6 engine, new exterior, new interior, and chassis updates. The new motor is another example of engine downsizing in the pickup truck industry. It replaced the 4.0L V6. Although the engine is smaller, it's stuffed full of the latest technology to offer good power and improved fuel efficiency. It features both direct and port fuel injection. It has an Atkinson cycle engine, which is usually reserved for smaller engines in Toyota's electric hybrid vehicles. It uses Toyota's variable valve timing technology and much more. The result is an engine that produces 278 horsepower at 6,000 RPM and 265 pound-foot of torque at 4,600 RPM. It represents a big 42 horsepower increase but a loss of 1 pound-foot when compared to the 4.0L V6 that preceded it.

The other big news is that the Tacoma switched from a 5-speed to a 6-speed automatic transmission. This contributes to an improved fuel economy and better use of the power under load.

We didn't know what to expect from the 2016 Tacoma on the grueling Ike Gauntlet test. When Toyota first introduced the redesigned Tacoma, they specifically said that towing prowess was low on the list of design requirements. The truck is more focused on off-road capability. Indeed, this Ike Gauntlet run was full of surprises.

We ran the previous generation 2015 Tacoma through the Ike Gauntlet with the same trailer just a year prior, so we had a solid basis for comparison. The Tacoma did not do well on the way down the mountain, but it beat all of our expectations on the way up!

We enabled Toyota's ECT PWR (Electronically Controlled Transmission Power) by hitting the button on the lower center console. Toyota's manual recommends using this setting when "driving in mountainous regions or when pulling a trailer." We were doing both, so better use this specially-designed transmission logic. Unfortunately, it did not offer grade shifting down the 7 percent grade of the Ike. Kent ended up hitting the brakes twenty-one times in order to maintain the 60 MPH speed limit down the mountain. This really hurt Tacoma's chances of winning this contest. The truck did great on the way up to the Continental Divide. It clocked in at 8:05 minutes, which meant it maintained the 60 MPH speed limit nearly the entire stretch of this 8-mile route. This is an impressive result, especially considering that the 2015 Tacoma ran the same test in 8:49 minutes. While the class winner, the 2016 GMC Canyon Diesel, took even longer up the same stretch at 8:55 minutes.

The 2016 Tacoma also impressed with a 4.5 MPG, as reported by its trip computer. This is a very good result for a naturally aspirated gasoline engine. Most gas-powered trucks cannot do better than 4.0 MPG up the Ike.

2016 GMC Canyon 2.8L Duramax Diesel (Chevy Colorado) [Ike Score: 87]

American truck enthusiasts had to wait no fewer than thirty-one years for a diesel-powered midsize pickup truck from General Motors. You could order a 1981 or 1982 Chevy LUV pickup with an optional Isuzu-sourced 2.2-L non-turbo diesel. This engine was also used in later Chevy S-10 and GMC S-15 pickups. The latter version of the engine produced 62 horsepower at 4,300 RPM and 96 pound-foot of torque at 2,200 RPM. This power output may be laughable by modern standards, but this was a reliable and efficient engine. I met an owner of a 1984 GMC S-15 diesel pickup in 2014. The truck had over 200,000 miles on the clock, and he was using it as a daily driver work truck for a home remodeling business. The little truck carried anything from gravel and cement, to lumber and tools. The owner claimed a stellar 31 MPG from the little diesel. Funny, we got 31.3 MPG from a 2016 GMC Canyon Diesel on our 100-mile highway efficiency test loop when running empty.

2.8L I4 & 6-speed Automatic transmission	181 hp at 3,400 RPM, 369 pound-foot at 2,000 RPM
Rear axle ratio	3.42
Towing party trick?	Torque, exhaust brake, grade shifting, trailer brake controller

The 2016 GMC Canyon Duramax with the 2.8L turbo-diesel was one of the most anticipated trucks of the year. This engine produces 181 horsepower at 3,400 RPM and 369 pound-foot of torque at 2,000 RPM. It is mated to a Hydra-Matic 6L50 6-speed automatic and a standard 3.42 rear axle ratio. The combination is good for an EPA-estimated 20 MPG in the city, 29 MPG on the highway, and 23 MPG combined. When launched, the truck was available in SLE and SLT Crew Cab models only. Shoppers who want the turbo-diesel over the V6 will need to pony up an additional $3,700 for a comparably equipped truck.

How would it do on the Ike? Would it embarrass most other trucks, or struggle to get up the mountain? The Canyon crushed every other truck we tested that year in downhill braking performance and uphill fuel efficiency. The "baby Duramax" registered just one brake application on the way down, and showed 6.7 MPG at the top of the mountain – the best efficiency reading we have ever seen. But it wasn't all roses and butterflies. The truck could not maintain the 60 MPH speed limit all the way up and clocked in at 8:55 minutes. It's not an awful time, but it is 50 seconds slower than the 2016 Tacoma with the same 5,600 pounds trailer.

This mid-sizer is bred to be a small towing machine. It is equipped with an integrated brake controller and an exhaust brake. These components are normally reserved for heavy-duty diesel pickups. This truck is a big HD pickup in a midsize package. The 6-speed transmission is well matched to the engine's output and the 3.42 rear-end ratio. These are the primary reasons why it did so well on the downhill and had such efficiency on the way up. It is also a stable and good-handling platform for towing medium-sized trailers. We tested it with up to 6,100 pounds of trailer, people, and cargo. Why was it slower than the competition on the way up? It may have to do with the relatively low horsepower rating (181 HP). Our testing has shown that trucks with lower horsepower outputs struggle to maintain the speed limit up the mountain and under load, even if they have lots of torque (like this 2.8-liter Duramax). If GM can squeeze 200 or 210 horsepower out of this engine, it would be an unstoppable small-towing machine.

With all this being said, the 2016 GMC Canyon Duramax won TFLtruck's 2016 Gold Hitch award for Truck of the Year. All of us have agreed that the small turbo-diesel engine in a midsize GM pickup truck is a great overall package with outstanding towing capability and efficiency. If there is a chink in its armor, it is the relatively high price. The 2016 Canyon Crew Cab 4x4 SLT we tested stickered at $44,365, including destination.

ANDRE

10

TOP 3
HD
IKE
GAUNTLET

BEST TOWING HEAVY DUTY PICKUPS ON THE MOUNTAIN

Finally... what about the big boys, the heavy-duty pickups? These are purpose-built towing and hauling machines. These are trucks you see hauling construction equipment and supplies around town or working the "hot shot" towing jobs on the highway.

The "big three" are in an all-out bare knuckle brawl against each other when it comes to HD trucks. It has been this way for decades, but the competition has intensified recently as the latest torque wars and towing/hauling ability wars are in full swing. Ford, General Motors, and Ram are bragging about their trucks' towing abilities, payload ratings, and horsepower and torque numbers. Each manufacturer is trying to one-up the others.

These are all Class 3 trucks with GVWR of up to 14,000 pounds.

	Max Payload	Max Bumper-pull Towing	Max Gooseneck Towing	GCWR
2016 Ford F-350 Crew Cab 4x4 Dually	**6,460 pounds**	19,000 pounds	26,500 pounds	35,000 pounds
2016 Chevy Silverado 3500 Crew Cab 4x4 Dually	5,743 pounds	**20,000 pounds**	22,600 pounds	31,100 pounds
2016 Ram 3500 Crew Cab 4x4 Dually	5,680 pounds	18,000 pounds	**30,310 pounds**	**39,100 pounds**

This table demonstrates that each manufacturer works hard to get even the slightest edge on competition. Each company can claim "best in class" in some category.

The question still remains: which one is the best towing heavy-duty pickup in the land? This is precisely why we load the trucks near their maximum capacities and head into the Rocky Mountains for the Ike Gauntlet.

What weight are we towing for the heavy-duty installment of the Ike Gauntlet? It is a 30-foot long gooseneck flatbed trailer loaded to 21,400 pounds. The total load on each truck, including people and gear, is 22,150 pounds.

You are probably already asking yourself why we are not towing a heavier load, since the Ram HD is rated at over 30,000 pounds of gooseneck towing. The answer is simple: the goal is to tow a weight that every competitor in the class is capable of towing safely, so it makes for a fair comparison across the board. This weight was chosen so that Ford, GM, and Ram could all safely tow it.

Power Wars

As of July 2016, this engine is the winner of the torque war among heavy-duty pickups. It's not the leader in the horsepower department. In it's the opposite. This engine is actually rated the lowest among the big three on horsepower. Naturally, the horsepower and torque wars will continue into the foreseeable future. The next generation of the Ford Super Duty will be rated close to 440 horsepower and 925 pound-foot of torque for the 2017 model year. Ford has just trumped Ram's 900 pound-foot of torque. Ram is likely to come back with an answer shortly. General Motors is also hard at work on their next generation of the Duramax V8. Who will reach the 1,000 pound-foot mark first? We will have to wait a little while longer to find out.

"$100,000 Pickup Truck?"

There surely will come a day when a fully-loaded HD pickup truck will cost $100,000. This day may not come in 2016 or 2017, but it is coming relatively soon. Ram is taking a step in this direction with an updated Limited trim package for 2016.

This is a top-of-the-line package with a new chrome grille design, big chrome "RAM" letters on the tailgate, additional chrome trim, and luxurious interior appointments that have a black, silver, and chrome theme. The 2016 Ram 3500 HD dually 4x4 Limited that we tested is stickered at $75,275. This is a truck that the boss drives, and the boss will likely use it as a tax write-off for the business.

2017 Ford Super Duty

Ford and General Motors are also moving in this direction. The 2016 Chevy Silverado 3500 dually 4x4 High Country edition that we tested listed at $69,915. The High Country package adds chrome exterior touches as well as interior upgrades. If the Chevrolet High Country is not to your liking, the GMC Sierra HD Denali might do the trick. A large percentage of the GMC HD pickup sales are adorned with Denali packages. A 2016 GMC HD Denali truck can get just beyond $70,000 with all the options. Ford is taking it to the next level with all-new 2017 Super Duty trucks. The next generation HD truck from Ford is completely redesigned and features an aluminum body and bed. It has many class-exclusive optional features, including adaptive cruise control and a panoramic sunroof. If you add all the options to a 2017 Super Duty F-450 dually 4x4 Platinum, then the final price will reach $88,605. This is as high as they get for now. Perhaps the $100,000 truck is several years away.

2.
2016 Ram 3500 HD Dually 6.7L Cummins I6
[Ike Score: 51]

The 2016 Ram 3500 HD can be optioned with a "high output" version of the 6.7L Cummins I6 engine that is rated at 385 horsepower at 2,800 RPM and 900 pound-foot of torque at 1,700 RPM. The dually 4x4 truck with the Limited package we tested had this motor and the heavy-duty 6-speed automatic Aisin transmission. This powertrain combination is only available in the Ram 3500 HD one ton trucks.

The Ram 2500 HD three-quarter ton trucks have two lower output Cummins engine options: one (with "only" 670 pound-foot of torque) mated to a 6-speed manual and the other (with "only" 800 pound-foot of torque) with a 6-speed automatic 68RFE transmission.

6.7L I6 & 6-speed Automatic transmission	385 hp at 2,800 RPM, 900 pound-foot at 1,700 RPM
Rear axle ratio	4.10
Towing party trick?	Over 30,000 pounds of towing capacity

Cummins-powered Ram heavy-duty trucks are equipped with an exhaust brake. An exhaust brake utilizes the geometry of the turbocharger vanes. When the driver lits off the throttle, the turbocharger vanes close and it provides engine back-pressure, which in turn helps to slow down the truck. There are two exhaust brake modes in the Ram: Auto mode that activates in a gradual way and is designed to maintain the truck's current speed on a downhill, and a Full/Regular mode that provides maximum braking assistance right away.

We used the Full/Regular exhaust brake mode on our way down the Ike Gauntlet mountain. We had to apply the brakes seven times on the way down. This represents a good performance on the downhill. The truck felt stable and confident down the mountain. You can actually hear the exhaust brake kicking on, which is re-assuring, considering this test is pushing over 31,000 pounds of

GCWR. The exhaust brake is not nearly as loud as on the big rig semi-trucks.

The Ram pulled strong up the mountain and clocked in at 9:58 minutes, which was 11 seconds quicker than the 2015 Ram 3500 dually with 865 pound-foot of torque. The extra power made the difference on the way up. The fuel economy at full throttle up the mountain was identical between the 2015 and 2016 versions of the big Ram. The trip computer reported 3.0 MPG, which is the best that we have seen when testing duallies at this weight.

There is no doubt that the Ram HD is a capable towing machine.

1.
2016 Chevrolet Silverado 3500 HD Dually 6.6L Duramax V8 [Ike Score: 56]

The 2016 Ram HD performed so well on the extreme test that it was difficult to imagine any truck could beat it. This is why we were surprised to see the 2016 Chevy Silverado HD take this win in the 2016 competition. [Note: We did not test 2016 Ford Super Duty, see below for results on the 2015 Super Duty.]

6.6L V8 & 6-speed Automatic transmission	397 hp at 3,000 RPM, 765 pound-foot at 1,600 RPM
Rear axle ratio	**3.73**
Towing party trick?	Downhill cruise control

The Chevy HD and GMC HD have the lowest maximum gooseneck towing rating and the lowest GCWR of the big three. It also has the lowest torque output of the three. The 6.6-liter Duramax V8 produces 397 horsepower at 3,000 RPM and 765 pound-foot of torque at 1,600 RPM. It is backed by a 6-speed Allison automatic transmission. GM is upgrading this engine for the 2017 model year, so it will be interesting to see how far they can push this setup. In the end, pure power numbers do not matter as much as hauling and towing capacities and real-world performance.

We tested the Chevrolet Silverado 3500 HD dually 4x4 High Country edition with Duramax power. The truck did an outstanding job down the mountain with just two brake applications. GM employs an interesting combination of diesel exhaust brake, transmission grade shifting logic, and an engine over-rev feature during downhill braking situations.

What is engine over-rev? The Duramax V8 has a redline at 3,450 RPM when the engine is on "powered" mode. Basically, when you are accelerating, the computer will enforce the 3,450 RPM limit. However, in "braking" mode when used during grade shifting, the computer can de-fuel the system and allow the engine over-rev up to 4,800 RPM to help slow the truck down. This is a high RPM count for any diesel, so don't worry if you see your Duramax jump to nearly 5,000 RPM on a downhill. The computer will take care of the engine.

The Chevy HD also impressed on the way up the mountain. The big Silverado went up in 9:48 minutes. This is 10 seconds quicker than the Ram HD. This is not a big margin, but part of the quicker time by Chevy can be explained by its higher horsepower rating. The Duramax V8 (at 397 HP) makes 12 more horsepower than the Cummin I6 in the Ram. This is also not a big difference, but the higher horsepower may have just a slight edge at keeping a higher speed on the steep stretches of the test.

Yes, you have probably guessed it by now: the quicker time up the mountain with the same load costs in efficiency. The Chevy HD registered 2.8 MPG on the uphill, versus 3.0 MPG in the Ram HD.

The Chevy was loaded very close to its maximum, and it performed exceptionally well. The ride was stable and relatively quiet. GM insulates the cabin and hushes down the engine better than most. There is no noticeable sound change when the exhaust brake engages. If the Ram HD's character is more brutish and truck-like, then the Chevrolet HD is more refined and calm.

Other Competition
Ford F-350 SD Dually 6.7L Power Stroke V8

Ford has refreshed the Super Duty for the 2015 model year with engine upgrades and interior tweaks. The company gave the truck a bigger turbocharger, an exhaust brake, and a fuel delivery system that is capable of delivering more fuel than before. Ford has taken a different approach to GM and Ram. Ford designs and builds their own heavy-duty turbo-diesel and transmission powertrain combination in-house. The upgraded 6.7-liter Power Stroke V8 produces 440 horsepower at 2,800 RPM and 860 pound-foot of torque at 1,600 RPM. This 2015 model year truck has a big horsepower advantage over the competition, although it does not quite match Ram's 900 pound-foot of torque.

This truck was towing a different gooseneck trailer, but basically the same weight. The orange trailer was loaded to 21,600 pounds and the total load was 22,350 pounds. It was towing a WWII 1942 M2 Halftrack military vehicle. We did not count the number of brake applications on the way down the mountain, but the Ford F-350 handled the descent without problems. The exhaust brake did its job, and was just loud enough to hear it kick in.

On the way up, the F-350 showed what horsepower can do for moving a heavily-loaded truck up the mountain. It clocked in at 9:44 minutes, which is the quickest time of the three, although the winning margin is just four seconds. All this power and a quick time cost in efficiency. The big Ford showed 2.7 MPG on the way up the Ike at full throttle and heavily loaded.

In the end, all three competitor heavy-duty trucks were remarkably close in their extreme towing performance. Still, a winner must be named, and it was the 2016 Chevy HD.

MR. TRUCK

11

UNDERSTANDING TRUCK AND TRAILER TIRES

TIRE RATINGS, SAFETY ISSUES

TRUCK TIRES

Tires are your first line of defense against the hard road. What many folks don't understand is what's printed in the truck owner's manual overrides what is stamped on the side of the tire just like it overrides the label on the receiver hitch. The truck and trailer manufacturers specify to the tire companies the load and performance parameters the tires must satisfy in order to be mated to the new trucks and trailers. The truck manufacturers decide and take responsibility for the load rating of the tire, as well as the required tire pressure. So check the owner's manual and the safety compliance sticker on the driver's door frame to see what your truck's tire pressure should be. Trailers also have a Safety Compliance Sticker that shows axle rating, tire weight rating, and air pressure. (According to the government, trucks include SUVs and minivans, so when I say "trucks," I cover the entire category.)

Which tire to get? If you're on a dry highway the majority of the time, simple highway tread works well with most trailer tires. But if you're on snow, ice, or pouring rain, then take a look at all-season and all-terrain tires. If you are a rock climber and sand jumper, then you're looking at wider tires with beadlock rims.

Are you confused yet? Some people under-inflate what the safety compliance door sticker states for tire pressure to get a softer ride. Low tire pressure causes the tire sidewalls to flex more and build up heat. Not a good thing. It works on an empty truck but not under a load. I would say stick to the air pressure ratings in the owner's manual and safety compliance door sticker. That's what's been tested to be safe. The maximum tire pressure should be measured with a cold tire. If the truck is sitting in the hot sun, or you've just driven a while, the tire will be in a "hot inflation" state, which could show 5 psi higher.

Some manufacturers have a different air pressure for the front truck tires versus the rears. A couple of years ago, Ram had a lower tire pressure setting you could use on heavy-duty trucks when empty. It would just lower the Tire Pressure Monitor to not beep or flash a warning in the dash. You still had to manually add or subtract air from the tires.

Half-ton trucks can have a P-rated tire for **"passenger tires."** Some have LT tires for *"light truck."* The Nissan Titan XD trucks have LT tires. All heavy-duty trucks — as in three-quarter ton and one-ton — have LT tires. LT tires can be 6-ply (C-rating), 8-ply (D-rating), 10-ply (E-rating), 12-ply (F-rating), and beyond.

You've heard of the Lincoln head on a penny measuring tire tread depth. Stick the penny in the tread head first, and if you see his whole head, the tire is illegally worn at 2/32-inch. Tires start at 10/32 or higher for snow tires. Truck tires need to be rotated every 5,000-6,000 miles.

On my rear wheel drive truck, I replace tires one axle at a time. Of course it's better to replace all four tires, but I lose tires to road conditions and I hate to buy four tires each time I blow one. So logically, I like to put the new tires on the front (steer axle) for better handling. But that would be a mistake. If you hit bad road conditions on a curve (water, snow, or ice) with good tires on the front and worn tires on the rear, the rear of your truck will break loose before the front. That's called a skid, or — for you enthusiasts — drifting. That's good on a track, but bad on a steep mountain road with 1,000 foot cliffs nearby.

TRAILER TIRES

Heat is the biggest enemy of trailer tires. Under-inflation is the second enemy, and it's related to heat. Running a heavier ply tire at the maximum tire pressure using nitrogen helps. Load rating per tires is stamped on the sidewall of the tire.

Trailer tires are ST for "specialty tire." ST tires have the same ply rating as truck tires. Something new is speed rating. My last three new trailers for 2016 have a speed rating on the side wall of the tire. My toy hauler RV trailer has an L rating for 75 MPH, my tilt trailer has an M rating for 80 MPH. For decades all ST trailer tires were speed-rated for only 65 MPH.

75 mph rating on the Trailer ST tire

In olden days, bias-ply were touted as the best trailer tires. They did have stiffer sidewalls, but flexing side walls helps the poor suspensions on trailers ride better. Radials produce less heat than bias-ply. Nowadays, radials rule just like they do in the truck world. Trailer tires are close together, throwing nails and debris at each other. Steel-belted tires can take lots of abuse from the road and nails before going flat. I use Slime on my trailer tires for even more protection. Eventually, when trailer tires have mandatory Tire Pressure Monitoring — available in aftermarket now — I'll have to quit using the thick, slimy stuff.

Back on the farm, when trucks had the same size tires as trailers, I would wear out tires on the truck and then run them on the trailer. Now, truck sizes have grown larger. And with my Commercial Driver's License (CDL) and DOT number, I have to follow the rules. I must be legal, so I use ST trailer tires. All tires need to be balanced. Trailer tires can be aligned and axles re-arched if you see excessive wear showing, excessive toe in or toe out, or wear on the inside of the tire. Over-inflation will wear the middle of the tires and under-inflation will wear the outsides. Some of you don't use your trailer often. After a few years, the tires have great tread but the side walls have dry rot from the sun. You can buy covers to protect the tires from direct sunlight.

Get a good tire pressure gauge. These are the long ones sold at better auto parts stores and truck stops. Cheap, short air pressure gauges are not accurate (or not accurate for long). If your truck has a factory tire pressure monitoring system (TPMS) and has individual pressure readings, it's interesting to watch the pressure go up when the tires warm up. You can even tell air pressure difference between the sunny side of your truck and the shady side. That tells you that heat expands the tires, increasing air pressure. This is why you want to check the air pressure before you drive when the tires are cool. If you check the tires when they are hot and let some of the air out to get the correct pressure, then when the tires cool down, they will be under-inflated. Trailer tires are basically the same as truck tires when it comes to proper air pressure. Look at the trailer owner's manual. Trailer manufacturers match tires like they do axles to be the proper combination for safety. With torsion axles, like the majority of horse trailers use, a flat tire may not feel much different. It can hang in position, so you could drive for miles with a flat and not know it until it destroys the tire and pieces are flying off the trailer, or when a flat tire tears apart and takes the trailer fender with it.

As mandated by law, newer trucks have tire pressure monitors as standard equipment. There are aftermarket tire pressure monitoring systems for trailers to keep tabs on the tire pressure on the go. Another value of having an onboard TPMS is being alerted that you have lost a tire or tire and wheel. It happens more often than you think. Tires will naturally lose air over time, making it important to check your tire pressures often. Using nitrogen instead of air is gaining popularity with over-the-road semi-trucks. It leaks less than air, collects less water inside the tire, and may make the tires last longer. It's also used in most race cars. If you blow one tire, it's usually better to replace both tires on the same axle. Don't use different sizes of tires on your trailer. Tire capacity on the axle must equal or exceed the axle weight rating. All the tires on the trailer should exceed the trailer GVW by 20 percent. Keep your trailer as level as possible for even wear on your tires and better braking.

If you blow a tire and drive it awhile, the other axle tire on the same side may get overloaded. Watch it closely or replace it. Even if you don't use your trailer much, three years in the sun may weaken the tires. I've towed 30,000 miles a year on trailer tires and got them to last two years. That's not normal; I'm a test dummy. It's more common for trailer tires to last less than 15,000 miles. The story is ST trailer tires are made heavier than even LT truck tires: heavier cords, greater tensile strength, and better chemicals in the rubber compounds. That's what tire companies will tell you. If that's the case, why can't you use them on trucks other than with traction issues?

If you rarely use your trailer, you can put the axles on blocks to take the weight off the tires or put plywood under the tire, lower the air pressure and put covers on them. Don't use the shiny stuff on the tires; it has alcohol. A trailer tire sitting for a long time can get a flat spot. Just like boats, guns, and engines, they last longer when they get used. (That's what she said.)

ST tires can be 6-ply (C-rating), 8-ply (D-rating), 10-ply (E-rating), 12-ply (F-rating) and beyond just like truck tires. On their large 30 foot Big Tex test trailer at TFLtruck.com, they have 16-ply H-rated tires. Triple axle tires on a trailer take special attention. Not just because the front and rear axle bearings can loosen up from all the tire flexing on corners, but also because the tire beads can lose air and the tire side walls can crack early. Bottom line is: take tires and tire pressures very seriously when truck'n and tow'n.

MR. TRUCK

TRUCK SAFETY

EXTRA TRUCK TIPS

Let's catch up on other important truck facts. Dually one-ton pickup trucks have their advantages for safely towing large trailers. I like them for trailers that are over 16,000 pounds. Having more tires on the ground helps handling on curves. It's also a bit better braking with six tires kissing pavement. The pivot with springs on an axle can be the same as a single rear wheel truck, meaning squat from the trailer tongue weight can be similar with just less tire squat. The down side is being eight feet wide, scraping fenders at the drive-through window, and trying to park at the mall. Not that I have done that. Duallies eat more fuel with the drag of extra tires.

Limited slip axles were the norm for pickup trucks. Now, you can have traction control and E-Locker differentials. Limited slip axle has a clutch in the differential (LSD). If the right tire slips, it engages the clutch so the left tire can join in. If you drive on slippery and loose surfaces often, it can wear out the clutch in the LSD. Traction control has been around for years on front-wheel drive cars. The ABS computer will brake the wheel that is slipping. Toyota used it on trucks first, but now it's common. E-Locker is my favorite because I can lock the axles together by pushing a button. I don't have to wear out a clutch, and I don't have to wait for it to engage.

Another reason to buy a new truck: you know what tire size came with it. In olden times, I mean thirty years ago, half-ton trucks had 15-inch tires. Then 16-inch tires, then 17-inch tires, and now 20-inch tires. Each size up, of course, costs more. I miss the 15-inch tires. The heavy duties with the larger size at least had a purpose. With 10-ply tires, going from 16-inch to 17-inch meant higher weight capacity. And a taller tire rolls easier, like the 24.5-inch on a semi-truck. Taller tires take more energy to start rolling, but once moving, the train keeps chugging along.

Weight Distributing Hitch

A WDH is important because it can improve how a half-ton handles with a trailer. Most truck manufacturers require it on trailers over 5,000 pounds. If it's required, it can affect your truck's warranty and your insurance claim.

GenY Hitch with WDH

To explain what a WDH does, think of it as a bridge between the towing vehicle and your trailer. This bridge comes complete with an adjustable under-truss called spring bar/arm, or trunnion bars, which join the "V" tongue of the trailer to the hitch head and receiver hitch that arch the bridge upward to spread out the load. The hitch head, with the trailer ball attached to the trailer coupler/hitch, bolts to the shank, which is an "L" shape, with adjustment holes for proper hitch height. The shank slides into your receiver hitch, which is bolted to the towing vehicle's frame or sub-frame. This union allows you to distribute the trailer weight evenly to all axles of the truck and trailer. Thus the name "weight distributing" hitch.

An important note here is that most vehicle manufacturers will only allow a maximum trailer capacity of 5,000 pounds' and 500 pounds' of tongue weight without using a weight distributing hitch. No WDH will increase the total trailer capacity set by the vehicle manufacturer, it just transfers the weight to all the axles including the front axle of your tow vehicle. This gives you better steering control and a level rig.

I adjust my WDH by feel, but you can weigh your truck empty and then weigh it with a trailer to get the trailer weight, then just weigh the truck on the scale with the trailer off the scale. That will tell you the tongue weight. Adjust your WDH for 10-15 percent tongue weight of your loaded trailer. If your WDH spring bars are too tight, then it is possible to move too much weight to the front axle and lose traction on your truck's rear axle on, say, a slippery boat ramp or mud and snow. Another rule of thumb is to measure the distance between your truck fender wells and tires without load and adjust the rear tire measurement (by adjusting the spring bars) to drop an inch lower than the front axle when loaded.

Sway control for WDH is mostly about friction. Something rubs on something else if the trailer moves side to side. This is to control how fast and how far the trailer pivots on the truck ball. By lifting the connecting point between the truck and trailer, tension is created. Add that to friction sway control and sway can be slowed down, but not eliminated. Don't forget what we covered in Chapter 4 about controlling trailer sway with the manual override on the trailer brake controller in your truck in an emergency.

Top Brands of WDH

Andersen WDH uses chains instead of spring arms and uses neoprene bushings to take the bounce out of driving, and has a beveled hitch head ball that is pushed down into a bushing for sway control.

Gen-Y Hitch is an adjustable receiver hitch that can have a WDH attached with one pin adjustment. The spring arms go from the hitch head to the bracket on the trailer tongue, with built-in sway control on the L-bracket on the trailer tongue providing friction.

Reese has several WDH hitches – the most common uses a trunnion arm with chains attaching to the trailer tongue brackets.

Old school WDH sway control is a sliding plate attached to the hitch head and trailer tongue with ball and socket. The slider has to be tightened to provide sway control friction, and it needs to be loosened in bad weather or when backing up. That wasn't very convenient.

A common WD hitch has a friction type anti-sway bar. But instructions may tell you to loosen the sway bar during rain or snow on some brands. That's when I want anti-sway the most. And, it has more bolts to drill into the trailer hitch. But this is the cheapest system of the three types of sway control.

The first place I remember seeing the WDH hitch was with folks pulling RV travel trailers, which used to be the gray-haired, retired, fixed-income conservative types. (Always watch this group, they seem to know something.) These big square travel trailers catch a lot of side wind and do the "Elvis pelvis" hip action when semi-trucks pass them. The RV world has embraced using WDH for decades for safety and handling reasons.

Horse trailers are the final frontier for broad use of the WDH. Hauling live, tall animals requires a WDH the most because of a high center of gravity. It would be the easiest place to see dramatic improvement: the WD hitches can add better steering control and braking than a level stable rig provides. I know it's one more thing to do when you hook up, and you may have to cut a slit in the nice tongue cover for the spring bar brackets, but it is an important safety measure. I applaud the horse trailer manufacturers who already have a boxed cutout in their tongues for a WDH. A good, properly adjusted WDH can take the sway, pitch and dip away from your trailer when trying to react to wind, semi-suction, potholes, and my favorite "swerving to miss the black Angus cow crossing the road at midnight."

You can't control the other drivers or debris in the road. So when you need to do those quick lane changes to avoid an accident, be sure your trailer will recover from that quick movement without taking you down the ditch and over. Horse trailers need it, boat trailers need it, and there's a reason so many RV travel trailers have them. I see more and more enclosed car haulers in Colorado using WD hitches. WDH can do more to safely level your sagging vehicle rear end than all the springs, shocks, and air bags combined. The WD hitch also places the trailer a few inches back to give you more room for a tight turn.

Trucks are getting longer rear springs for a better ride, but that can mean more rear end sag. SUVs have mostly gone to independent rear axles and coil springs, replacing leaf springs. This can create more sway, increasing the need for weight distributing hitches.

A level load will allow all of your brakes, wheel bearings, springs, and tires to help with the load. As with all the capacity maximum factory ratings, the GAWR can't be changed. They are set by the manufacturer, and are considered the rule. If the rig pulls well, then you are close to balanced. Since the GAWR can't be changed, use the spring bars to move weight between the tow vehicle's axles. You can lift the spring bars on your WDH a notch before you weigh it again. Lifting the spring bar (trunnion bar) will transfer some weight to the front axle. But if you move too much weight forward you can lose traction on the rear axle. So that's the adjustment you have to fine tune. You can add air shocks or overload springs, etc., if you want more support on the rear axle, though none of that will increase the capacity. But the WDH adjustment is the best thing to do for supporting the weight. Adding springs, shocks, air bags, etc., doesn't change the GAWR or any of the weight ratings, which is why I believe the WDH is the best trailer tool for a half-ton truck. The axle ratings on the door tag is the maximum for each axle that you want to be under.

The truck below needs a WDH. It's sagging too much and is not level. The trailer brakes won't work as well and the truck axles will be overloaded.

Using the trailer jack to lift up the trailer tongue can help when attaching the spring bars to the trailer tongue chains or brackets. The same thing can help take the pressure off the spring bars when unhooking.

The trend is using the independent rear suspensions coming from the SUVs and crossovers. They ride great, but all that extra movement for the soft ride will let a trailer move more. The coil spring suspensions found on most SUVs also allow more trailer sway, so I highly recommend using a WDH. The better ones are easy and fast to hook up. Watch the retired gray hairs pulling RV travel trailers; 80 percent of them will have a WDH. And their cargo doesn't shift weight from one hoof to the other when swatting flies with its tail.

I relate most of my towing experiences with going up and down hills. We have some tall hills in Colorado with snow still on them in the summer. Going downhill with a trailer pushing you and trying to steer you can get spooky. You will see semi-trucks adjust their weight with sliding fifth wheel hitches and sometimes sliding trailer axles. This is a good idea for your trailer, also. Being able to adjust where the weight is distributed on your truck and trailer will give you a level rig, allowing all the axles and brakes to work for you.

Bed Liners, Resale, and Safety

I was surprised when I moved to Denver to sell trucks and saw used five-year-old pickups with beds that looked new. After I dropped the first salt block and 1,500 pound big round bale in the bed, my trucks on my farm-ranch just didn't look the same. The tailgate was left smiling. But that's where bed liners come in. They can keep the dents from lowering your resale value. If you don't haul a fuel tank or fuel containers in your truck bed, then the cheaper plastic bed liners will work. If you haul fuel cells or fuel containers, then you are better with a sprayed-in bed liner or nothing at all. I'm not talking about the used trucks where the dealer put the slide-in bed liner in to hide where the gooseneck hitch was, like we talked about in Chapter 6.

With slide-in plastic bed liners, you want to be careful with fuel containers. There is a gap between the bed liner and the pickup sheet metal floor where static electricity can build up. Almost none of the documented incidents of gas fires involve direct fueling of a truck because both vehicles and dispensers are designed to take static electricity to the ground. Instead, they involve gas stations where the gas can was in the bed and the driver was on the ground pouring gas in the can. Now, gas pumps have warning signs about taking the gas can out of the truck and putting on the ground before you fill it.

Gasoline does not conduct electricity very well. As a result, a charge of static electricity builds up on gasoline as it flows through a hose and this charge takes several seconds to several minutes to leave after the gasoline has reached a gas tank. If this charge discharges as a spark from a gas can to the grounded metal nozzle of the gas-oline dispenser hose, it may ignite the gasoline. Ignition requires that the spark occur near the tank opening where the gasoline vapor is flammable. A spark discharge directly from the surface of the gasoline to the grounded nozzle also can happen. This is the situation that happens when a metal container is placed on a plastic drop-in bedliner. The slower gasoline flows, the less static electricity is generated.

It seems that sprayed-in bedliners are one of the most popular truck options I see today. The first two things I do to a new truck is to get a sprayed-in bedliner and gooseneck hitch. You do want to have the sprayed-in liner done by someone with experience. Out here in Colorado, a lot of dealers are buying their own machines to spray in the bed liners. A lot of those dealers have no experience, and they are making a mess of things by making the bed liners too soft, too thin, and more. What I would do is have the operator who sprays your bed take out the tailgate bolts and the inside cargo bolts. On a Ford, I have them tape off the bed bolts. If you ever have to work on the tailgate latch and don't tape off the bolts or take them out, then you will have to chisel that stuff off. To get the bed off in the case of changing the fuel pump in the fuel tank of a Ford, you don't want to have to chisel that bed liner off all eight bolts. Don't get rushed into buying a sprayed-in bed liner when you buy the truck unless you have already done your research and know the right price and brand that you want. It's becoming more common to have a factory sprayed-in bedliner in a new truck. Nissan had the first factory sprayed-in bedliner when the Titan was born in 2002. I've sold trucks out in the country that spend a lot of time on dirt roads like my trucks did. We sprayed the liner on the lower rocker panels, and it does stop the pitting from gravel and lowers some of the noise. Under-coating is use-ful on dirt roads too, but don't pay hundreds for a $3 can. With stainless steel exhaust and plastic fuel tanks, there is only sheet metal you want to undercoat. Don't spray the driveline. You'd be surprised how little gets sprayed when you have a dealer do it. But spraying the sheet metal has a big benefit, especially on dirt roads.

The Federal Magnuson-Moss Consumer Warranty Act of 1975: Does Not Apply to Leased Vehicles

Have you heard of this law? In olden days, new truck dealers would try to void your factory warranty if you added a cold air intake or anything. Grease Monkey will post this law on the wall in their service centers. I've seen it posted in progressive new truck service centers. Look it up, but basically it states you can improve your truck as long as you don't mess up the pollution controls or cause something else to break on the truck. Also, the new truck dealer has to give you in writing what failure they can prove your after-market accessory caused.

This law is important. It also covers your rights on warranties. If a warranty is offered, you don't have to earn it or fill out a card and send it in for it to be in effect. Filling out warranty cards is a marketing gimmick to get your information to send you more marketing crap.

Crossing the safety chains can cradle the trailer coupler if it drops, allowing you to use your trailer brake controller to control the trailer as you pull off to the side of the road. This happened to me when I failed to latch the coupler in the rain.

CDL and Other Stupid Laws

If you think you're confused about trailer laws, ask the Department of Transportation!

OK, it's not a stupid law, it's just confusing, and all states don't look at it the same. (Some require class A and other licenses for towing trailers.) The CDL law that was supposed to stop the confusion between states is not consistent. First, I got the DOT number and the Colorado State Patrol inspection. Then, I took at least 6 CDL tests on the Motor Vehicle computer. Then, I went to a CDL school to pay $150 to take the driving test.

I don't agree with some of the questions on the tests about using the independent trailer brake just for testing trailer brakes at the start of the day, but it does teach you to look ahead on the road to avoid obstacles, reading all the signs, and watching the truck gauges. I had a Class A on the farm, but it didn't get grandfathered in when I moved to the city. That was a mistake. The written test wasn't bad: lots of questions about air brakes. I got the endorsement for multiple trailers. The driving test was hard. Had to parallel park the trailer, and the test dude had me drive through miles of construction. He would ask me what the sign said five miles back. If you stepped the trailer over a curb or line, you were automatically done and had to retake the test. I didn't cross the lines, but I did button-hook turns to drive past the lane and swing back in. He took off points for that. I passed. He said I was the first driver he passed. Of course I had my John Wayne gangster look going.

I've been interviewed several times about CDL laws, and I never meant to write about it because of the confusing inconsistent rules in different states. DOT publishes the book each month with all the new rules. It looks like a dictionary. Someday I'm going to read it. You'll want to do your own research with CDL, DOT, and state trailer laws. The state laws on trailers are worse on the coasts, like in California and all those little states on the East Coast.

The basic rules are: if you use your truck and trailer to make money, then the DOT wants you to have a DOT number and inspections if your Gross Combined Weight Rating is 10,001 pounds. You need to keep a logbook and inspection book. It's almost the same rules as CDL. A CDL license in its most basic rules means towing over 26,001 pounds of GCWR. This pertains to you if you are making money with your truck or thinking about making money with your rig.

Farmers are exempt from these rules if they are driving less than 150 miles from their farm. Ranchers are also exempt in most states except California. There are also Interstate rules and Intrastate rules and annual inspections for your truck and trailer. The log books are not a big deal. You use them to keep track of your time on the road. You may need it to track your mileage anyway for the tax deduction. The inspection book has a list of what to check on your truck and trailer. If you are driving within 150 miles of your truck office, then you don't have to fill out the log books on the road, but you are supposed to log this in your office books. If you're healthy, you only have to have a physical every couple years for your CDL. I have the physical every year because a previous physical discovered my high blood pressure.

For everyone else: either get a ranch or a farm, or get a CDL license and buy a log book. Starting in 2011, all one-ton duallies have a Gross Combined Weight Rating of at least 30,000 pounds., creating the possibility of needing a CDL license with a dually towing a trailer.

Since the DOT doesn't enforce the rules the same from state to state, you should protect your driver's license. The one thing the DOT does agree on is RVs. Pull a fifth wheel RV or a horse trailer with Living Quarters and I haven't seen where they require a CDL or logbook. (Is that a loophole?) A Living Quarters in your horse trailer — like an RV trailer — may be considered a second home or a vacation home, and interest may be tax deductible. Check with your accountant.

If you do haul into other states, getting a CDL might save some headaches later. Truck manufacturers are taking turns putting out more power from the diesels. Trailer manufacturers in turn are making bigger trailers. Here in Colorado, the mountains cause some unique problems with big trailers chasing you down the fast side of the mountain. I would think some education about driving and controlling one of these bigger rigs may be a good idea. We have laws about wearing seat belts and having airbags and ABS brakes on trucks over 10,000 GVWR. In the mountains, our only protection from inexperienced drivers losing control of a 3/4-ton truck pulling a 20,000 trailer or a 40 foot Class A motorhome is the runaway ramp on the side of the road. But don't do it! Those runaway ramps are made to slow down an 80,000 lb. semi-truck.

I've pulled some big trailers at night in the mountains, and between dodging the deer, I was keeping track of where the next runaway ramp was located, just in case.

Learn What the Government Knows and Visit these Sites!

US DOT: http://www.dot.gov

Federal Highway Admin: (FHWA) http://fhwa.dot.gov

Federal Motor Carrier Safety Admin: http://fmcsa.dot.gov

Goosenecks tow easier than bumper pull trailers (conventionally) and they back up slower and easier. The trailer tongue weight is distributed more evenly. Look at the massive safety chains.

Protect your Kids from the Dangerous Roads

1. I was glad my sons and I learned to drive on the farm.

2. A pickup holds very few friends.

3. What will they use to move to college?

4. A pickup could be their second vehicle for decades.

#1 My sons learn to drive

I remember driving tractors when I was 10 years old: our "53" Ford F250 and then onto the two-ton "47" Chevy truck. Clutches were fun. Dad called my learning curve "jackrabbit starts." There were a few times when we hauled bales from the field when I was driving, and my dad and my brother were loading the bales as I drove along with the "Graves bale loader." Some of my "jackrabbit starts" flipped my brother off the back of the truck seven bales high! He was not happy with his little brother. This might have been one of the reasons I went to big round bales when I had the farm (along with the fact that you can find sandburs, cockleburs, and rattlesnakes stuck in the little bales). But I was glad I learned to drive on the farm with all the room in the pasture to practice.

My sons learned to drive in the same pastures and fields. They discovered the same things about clutches. I think I yelled at them the same as my dad yelled at me. We all want our kids to be safe, and driving is a very dangerous thing, especially when we are young and prone to showing off. My boys followed me in the small pickups (Ranger, Mazda) behind the tractor and baler. This makes the top speed 18 MPH when following a tractor, a good speed to learn and daydream. Some of the dirt road hills did test the clutch skills and made for some "jackrabbit starts." A few times turning corners seemed challenging, watching the boys drive straight into the ditch instead of the turn. Watching my boys drive the '77 Chevy dually was always fun.

It took both of them to push in the clutch just to start it. The old Chevy had a 4.55 rear axle ratio, so it did take off well. But I use to love to watch my boys' heads bob up and down above the steering wheel as they pushed in the clutch. The next battle was my oldest son's 1970 Malibu. The gears were very close and first gear was hard to find, but he did find all the gears, especially the "go fast" one.

#2 A pickup holds very few friends

A regular cab truck, with only three seat belts, makes it hard to fill it full of friends. Not to mention, there's no back seat, which can create all kinds of havoc. Trucks don't usually have the top speed of a muscle car. I know from experience that no matter how many speeches you give your kids, they try to find the car's top speed when given the chance. That might explain why my dad bought a straight-6 in my first car instead of a V-8. I still managed to get that car to 90 MPH, though!

As mentioned earlier, my oldest son's Malibu, after he found all the gears, reached the top end once or twice. After that, he had to save up his money for a new engine. But the cars my sons had seemed to hold their whole high school class! I don't understand it. But a pickup, especially one with a floor shift, held a lot fewer friends.

#3 The College move

And the move from college dorm to apartment to apartment and, someday, to a house is where the truck has no equal. I lost track of how many times we moved before our second son was born. Your children can also be very popular with a truck, since they have the ability to help their classmates with college events.

You've all heard of the company "Two Students and a Truck." There you go: the part-time job besides delivering papers, pizza, and the lawn mower. The insurance cost is generally lower for a pickup than a muscle car, and it looks better than a four-door family car to their friends.

#4 The truck that lasts forever

If your children don't trade off their trusty truck, it could last for your grandchildren. I have had some thirty-year-old trucks. Pickup trucks are a body on frame construction. The frames hold the body together, give it strength, and contain the impact in an accident. The sheet metal is usually thicker on a truck than a car. Also, the resale value is better for a truck than a car.

I recommend a full-size truck (Ford F150, Ram 1500, GM 1500, Toyota Tundra). This size gives you the protection and capacity. If your kids keep the truck, they are always needed for hauling carpet, appliances, wood, garage sales, and lawn mowers. Oh hey, they could bring their lawn mowers over to your house when you are too old to mow, or at least when you are retired and running around in your RV.

Just for safety reasons, the pickup trucks are generally taller than the crowd of cars, giving you better visibility and an advantage in an accident. In the big city where I live now, I see kids constantly in accidents. It's not an easy task driving and growing up. I wish all kids could learn in the pasture that I did. Car crashes remain the number one killer of our teens. Before ending up with dead teenagers, first try learning by driving on dirt roads.

I grew up driving on gravel roads. Gravel gave you traction on wet roads, but the gravel would form ribbons like ruts that would steer your truck. The most dangerous part of the country dirt (gravel) road is the soft shoulder. Both of my sons had classmates who died on dirt roads because of the soft shoulder.

I took my sons, daughters, and grandkids to learn how to drive on dirt roads. I showed them how, when the shoulder pulls you in, you should just drive on down the ditch. You might get stuck in the ditch, but the tow truck is a better sight than the ambulance.

Rural Roads are dangerous because:

1. Farm machinery can be wide and take up the whole road. Pop over a hill and there it is: a 30-foot combine, 20-foot tractor, or 18-foot swather. It takes longer to stop on a dirt road.

2. No license: young drivers on the farm start early. I was twelve when I started driving on the farm.

3. Riding in the back of pickup.

4. Railroad crossings.

5. Soft shoulders, ruts, potholes, and washboard surfaces all are found on dirt roads. It's like driving on a battlefield.

6. Growing up in the country and driving on gravel roads most of my life gave me a unique way of evaluating how trucks and the accessories perform on dirt roads, as well as on asphalt. The correct wheel tracking will make a difference you can feel.

My daughters, at sixteen, wanted a manual-shift car. Someday I'll teach them how to shift. But we bought them both Ford Escorts with automatic transmissions. I know it's fun to shift gears and play NASCAR, but I know teenagers. Between talking to friends, talking on the cell phone, fixing makeup, watching boys drive by and drinking Mountain Dew, which hand would be free to shift? Also, where is the coordination to push the clutch, find the right gear, hit the brake, and accelerate? Just learning to steer, accelerate, and brake was enough. Teenage years are full of distractions, there will be time to learn to shift after college.

MR. TRUCK

13

CUSTOMIZING YOUR RIDE

MR. TRUCK

OUR TOP TRUCK & TRAILERING ACCESSORIES TO CUSTOMIZE YOUR RIDE

Top 5 Truck Accessories
(More folks buy accessories for their new trucks than for used trucks)

1. Tonneau Cover

2. Sprayed-in Bedliners

3. Custom Wheels

4. Exhaust

5. Centramatic wheel balancers. Famous on big rigs, they work on trailers, too.

Top 5 Trailering Accessories That Make a Difference

1. Gooseneck extension

2. Mudflaps or Rock Guards

3. Adjustable Receiver Hitch

4. Extra Fuel Tank

5. Cameras

Top 5 Off-Road Truck Accessories
(this category goes for functional upgrades)

1. Tires and bead locks

2. Winch

3. Floor mats that hold mud and slush

4. Cold Air Intake

5. Suspension including lift kits

Fading Favorites
(truck manufacturers watch trends and then capitalize by offering the top accessories as new truck options.)

1. LED lighting, on outside, in the bed

2. Trailer Brake Controllers

3. Gooseneck Hitch

4. Running boards

5. Navigation

Top 5 Truck Accessories:

1. Tonneau cover: This is #1 on most lists, because you need to protect what's in your bed and be able to lock it. When it's a factory truck option, we're told it can improve fuel mileage. That's believable. I like the hard top rolling or sliding. The soft tops are more popular and cheaper, but I've had them fly straight up coming out of the Ike Tunnel in Colorado from the suction. That's what she said.

2. Sprayed-in bedliners: We've covered this in Chapter 12: it's the first thing I do to a new truck. You'd be surprised how thin new truck bed sheet metal is. It was thick back in 1972, then they went to shit. Now, besides protecting the bed, making it less slick, and helping resale value, it adds structural integrity by doubling the thickness of the bed floor. Someday this will be on the "Fading Favorites" list because it is an option on most new trucks.

3. Custom wheels: Yes, the new trucks come with cool wheels that work for a tight-ass like me. Who doesn't like an awesome chrome wheel with black inserts, gray borders, a red strip around the rim, and beauty rings and….I add custom wheels to my trailers and ATVs, which makes a big difference in photos. I painted the wheels on my 1970 C10 Chevy restore project, but I will get gray spoke wheels for it, like in *Bullet* with Steve McQueen.

4. Exhaust: This would fit all the categories, but it's one of the top accessories truck owners get first. It adds power and helps the engine breathe for less engine heat, which all helps if you add a chip or programmer to your truck.

It could even improve MPG. But we know why you want it. It's that cool sound that nothing beats, especially on a V-8. Add headers and you're a hot rod. (That's what she said.)

5. *Centramatic wheel balancers:* Instead of a category, I've named this by brand because there are very few companies. All tires need balance. The first company that sold balancers was started in the '70s by J.C. Whitney. They made a ring that clamped on your hub cap. Now, balancers are a ring that goes on your wheel studs. BBs in the ring, damped with synthetic oil, balancing everything in the circle, including: wheel bearings, brakes, tires, wheels, etc. There's even a model for motorcycles. Prop airplanes use a version of it. Walk through a truck stop and look for the silver rings behind the chrome 24.5-inch wheels on semi-trucks.

Centramatic Wheel Balancer

Top 5 Trailering Accessories That Make a Difference

1. *Gooseneck extension:* The #1 selling truck for over a decade is, of course, a crew cab short bed. But trailer companies haven't heard yet. The majority of gooseneck and mini fifth wheel trailers aren't made for short bed trucks. This has opened a whole industry of gooseneck extensions and sliding 5th wheels. You want to look at this before you break your truck's rear window. Some trucks have a bigger blind spot looking out the back corner. Backing up a trailer gets you in more trouble than turning corners. Test jack knife your trailer before you hit the road.

2. Mudflaps or rock guards: It's not the rocks that cause the most damage to your trailer, it's the little BB-size pebbles that are thrown from your truck tires at 70 MPH. That's why the gelcoat on boats and RVs doesn't look so pretty after a couple of years. There are good mudflaps that point down at 70 MPH and guards that fit your truck's fender wells. In my youth, we bolted mudflaps on the rear bumper. Now you can get them to fit your receiver hitch. There is a reason why semi-trucks are required to have mudflaps.

3. Adjustable receiver hitch: You need a hitch anyway. Unless you only tow one trailer forever, having a hitch that will adapt to different trailer heights is important. It's important to keep your trailer level. This maximizes the trailer brakes, suspension, and wheel bearings.

4. Extra fuel tank: If you tow cross country, you'll wish you had more fuel. Some states like Missouri and Oklahoma have the cheapest fuel in the nation. Michigan and California are on the higher end. With GPS and navigation, you can find the cheapest fuel on your route and top off your tanks. Aftermarket tanks can be in your bed or down between the frame. This is the kind of accessory I like that can pay for itself with fuel cost per mile.

5. Cameras: This will head to the Fading Favorites too, with factory cameras around the corner. GM has a wireless trailer camera option on Heavy Duties for 2016. Ford 2017 Super Duties have seven cameras as an option with a corded camera for the trailer. But FCC rules will only let factory cameras used for backing up in the cab. GM has a camera under the mirror that works for blind spots when you use the turn signal. I use wireless cameras now. It's hard to see around an 8-foot-6-inch trailer with just trailer mirrors. And aftermarket cameras can stay on, so you can watch cars directly behind your trailer.

Top 5 Off-Road Truck Accessories
(this category goes for functional upgrades)

1. Tires: Besides wearing them out, we all like big tires. Off-road use makes for tough tires and sometimes bead locks. Use deep tread or wide low pressure tires for your favorite off-road exploring. Many trucks available are for dual purpose: daily driver and weekend warrior. Why not two sets of tires and wheels? It's nothing to change wheels, Nascar does it several times a race. You just need a floor jack and a good cordless impact wrench.

2. Winch: Having a winch to get unstuck solves some embarrassing situations. And you can explore deeper into the abyss. Be the hero when your friends get stuck. I seem to drive in blizzards when I don't intend to. I have a winch.

3. Floor mats: Floor mats have come a long way. Now you can order them to fit your truck floor exactly and even hold water. Replacing your truck's carpet is a pain in the....I seem to be in the mud too much in the spring and usually drag it into my truck. Keep your carpet in good shape and that should be worth a little more at resale time. Trying to vacuum dried mud in the carpet doesn't work. My truck has a rubber floor but I still have mats.

4. Cold air intake: A very popular accessory for some power. More air for your engine is a good thing. It's an easy install and usually you can feel and hear the difference. The air filters can be paper-or oil-embedded cloth which last longer than factory air filters.

5. Suspension including lift kits: This is an expensive option. But if you're serious about off-roading, lifting your truck with taller tires will give you more ground clearance. And it looks cool, climbing up into your truck with a rope. Chicks dig tall trucks. Suspension can be air bags, longer torsion bars, and double shocks with an oil reservoir all for more wheel travel.

Fading Favorites: Truck manufacturers watch trends and then capitalize by offering the top accessories as new truck options.

1. LED lighting: New trucks are covered in LED lights, around headlights, tail lights, and in the bed. But you can buy stacked LED headlights for your used truck. LEDs use very little juice when you add them inside your bed, under your running boards, and under your dash. Using red and green lights close to the floor can keep your peripheral vision going, moving your eyes, and can help keep you awake. There's a reason aircraft gauges are red. Guys who put multi-color LEDs around their frames and axles to light up the undercarriage are an exception.

2. Trailer brake controllers: Take some time and get a good one that is proportional. Most truck manufacturers offer them integrated. Just a few midsize trucks and SUVs don't have them yet, but it won't be long. Not all factory brake controllers are created equal. The good news is that they can be replaced with a better aftermarket trailer brake controller.

3. Gooseneck hitch: Again, popular as factory options on heavy-duty trucks, which takes the hassle out of having them installed. As with most factory options, they are more expensive than aftermarket brands. I'm kind of on the fence. I like the aftermarket gooseneck hitches that I can turn over and put the greasy ball back in the hole for a flat, usable truck bed. Factory gooseneck balls have to come out and go into a bag with plastic covers for the hole and safety chain pucks.

4. Running boards: With tall 4x4 trucks, running boards will save your butt and shins. Yes, the factories figured that out, too. I don't understand all the new running boards that pop out of the side of the bed or swing forward and back to reach the bed. I like a long running board that goes from fender to fender. Then I can reach the aftermarket cross-over tool box.

5. Navigation: Remember Garmin or TomTom? Now phones have it. New trucks have some awesome navigation and info-tainment systems on 8-inch screens in the dash that talk to you and expect you to talk back. You would have to work hard to get lost. The big screen doubles for the backup camera or 360 cameras, which is a great bonus. Below, trailers, trailers and trailers. Between TFLtruck.com and MrTruck.com we have seven new test trailers, seven WDH hitches, and nine adjustable receiver hitches. That's a lot of greasy balls!

ANDRE

14

GOING OFF THE BEATEN PATH

BEST OFF-ROAD PICKUP TRUCKS

A huge part of the pickup truck experience is going where the pavement ends. This is all about freedom and the American spirit. It's about going wherever you want and whenever you want.

Kent and I, and the rest of the TFLtruck.com and MrTruck.com crew live in Colorado, at the foot of the Rocky Mountains and the Continental Divide. There are more mountain 4x4 trails and farm roads of the high plains than a person can explore in a lifetime.

Part of the off-road experience is the fun of it: spending the weekend with your buddies at a remote camping site above tree line or going for an afternoon of trail running. The flip side of the coin is all about serious business. Thousands of hardworking guys and gals across the country must deal with mud, dirt, and rocks on a regular basis as part of their job. I am talking about park service, fire fighters, law enforcement, construction, oil and gas, waste management, farming, logging, mining, and many more industries. These jobs can be fun, but they can also be very tough. Having the right truck for the job is important.

Which off-road truck to get? Every pickup truck manufacturer in the United States has an off-road focused pickup truck offering. We have tested them all on the Rocky Mountain trails (see Chapter 2 for description of our off-road tests). In the end, only one truck can be the Gold Hitch Truck of the Year, but it's worth considering the competition. The 2016 Off-Road Truck of the Year will be unveiled at the end of this Chapter.

We use these five criteria to evaluate each truck's off-road worthiness. Keep these in mind as we move on to the best off-road truck for 2016.

- **Tires**
- **Ground clearance, approach/departure/breakover angles**
- **AWD / 4x4 system traction management**
- **Suspension articulation and comfort**
- **Power delivery**

The ultimate off-road truck would have the most aggressive and specially-designed off-road tires, highest clearance, largest approach/departure/breakover angles, a 4x4 system that offers low range gearing and allows for all wheels to claw at the earth at the same time, great articulation to keep the tires on the ground for ultimate traction, and good power to get up and over a ledge or steep hill.

Let's tackle all of the off-road pickups in alphabetical order, and finally get to the off-road truck of the year.

All of the ground clearance and angles are listed for crew cab 4x4 trucks with the shortest available bed. Also, some manufacturers measure or report ground clearance in different ways. Some report the clearance between the ground and the bottom of each differential, others report "running ground clearance." The numbers listed here are all the minimum listed, or the smallest ground clearance listed by each manufacture for the 4x4 versions of their trucks.

Chevrolet Colorado Z71 (Trail Boss Edition)

	Ground Clearance	Approach Angle	Breakover Angle	Departure Angle
Chevy Colorado Crew Cab 4x4	8.2 in	17.3 deg	19.8 deg	22.1 deg

The Z71 is a well-known Chevy truck and SUV trim package. In recent years, Z71 brand stands for off-road focused performance at Chevrolet. In the case of the midsize Colorado pickup, the Z71 package adds unique styling touches, capable all-terrain tires, and the mechanical components and hardware to back up the more rugged look. The Z71 package offers an automatically locking rear differential, hill descent control, specially-tuned off-road suspension, and additional underbody protection. These are all the good things for off-roading.

The locking rear differential can detect a speed differential between the two rear wheels, and if one wheel is way faster (spinning freely in the air as the truck is flexing over obstacles) the system locks the two axle half-shafts so both wheels can propel the truck through the slippery situation. This is also very helpful on snow, ice, or other low-friction surfaces.

The Hill Descent Control feature uses the truck's antilock braking system to help provide a slow and controlled descent in off-road situations. It is driver-activated with a push of a button, and it works without the driver pressing on the brake pedal. This system is not new to SUVs or off-road oriented crossovers, but it's only recently started to proliferate across the pickup truck segment. Even a driver who is well-versed in this system takes a small leap of faith when going down an exceedingly steep hill without pressing on the brake pedal. It's a bit similar to riding a roller coaster.

There is one not-so-good element that comes with every Chevy Colorado. It is the front spoiler (or air deflector) that is mounted underneath the front bumper. It is there to improve aerodynamics of the truck at highway speed. While this is a good thing for long highway runs, it limits the approach angle on the Chevy Colorado. It is still there when you order the Z71 and the Trail Boss packages. Chevrolet says that the air deflector is easily removable. It is removable, but it will take some time. There are more than a dozen mounting screws, and some of them are not easy to get to.

The Trail Boss Edition is the next step up the off-roadability ladder for the Colorado pickup. It adds aggressive off-road Goodyear Wrangler Duratrac tires as well as a sport bar behind the cab with additional LED lights mounted up high, unique side assist steps, fender flares, and several other cosmetic touches and badges. This is all great, except the assist steps take away some of the ground clearance and could scrape. Yes, they can help protect the body of the truck against trail damage, but they hang relatively low.

The Chevy Colorado with the Z71 or the Z71 Trail Boss package is a midsize pickup with good off-road capability. Removing the front air deflector and the side steps would further improve its off-road performance. We have taken the Colorado Z71 Trail Boss up the gorgeous Argentine Pass in Colorado. It performed very well. We returned in one piece, but we wished we had just a little more ground clearance and a better approach angle.

Rumors are still swirling around the future availability of a Colorado ZR2 model, the ultimate midsize off-road truck from Chevrolet. It is still not officially confirmed as of this writing.

Chevrolet Silverado Z71

	Ground Clearance	Approach Angle	Breakover Angle	Departure Angle
Chevy Silverado Crew Cab 4x4	8.9 in	18 deg	19 deg	23.2 deg

The Z71 off-road package is also available on the full-size Chevy Silverado light-duty and heavy-duty pickup trucks. The recipe is basically the same as in the Colorado Z71. It combines the same ingredients in a bigger truck to improve off-road capability. It includes the specially-tuned suspension, all-terrain tires, hill descent control, and automatically locking rear differential.

Silverado heavy-duty trucks are also offered with the Z71 package. I must note that the Rancho shocks and off-road tuned suspension on the Silverado HD trucks offer the best on-road ride in the segment, empty or loaded. It's not ideal for towing heavy trailers, or running near maximum payload capacity, because of the extra side-to-side movement of the suspension. Still, the Chevy HD truck with the Z71 suspension runs smoothly over rough paved roads like a ligh-duty truck would. That is a big plus in my book.

The Z71 package works well for the Silverado. The suspension offers good articulation, especially at the rear axle. The verdict is similar to the Colorado Z71. We have driven the off-road version of the Silverado on the mountain trails of Colorado and Nevada. The truck performed well in all our off-roading, but we never took it on a trail of high difficulty, primarily due to relatively low ground clearance and approach/departure angles that are not meant for extreme off-roading.

GMC Canyon All-Terrain and the **GMC Sierra All-Terrain** are configured in basically the same way as the Chevy Colorado Z71 and Chevy Silverado Z71 trucks.

Ford F-Series FX4

	Ground Clearance	Approach Angle	Breakover Angle	Departure Angle
Ford F-150 Crew Cab 4x4	9.4 in	25.5 deg	21 deg	26 deg

Ford F-Series FX4

The Ford truck FX4 Off-Road package is designed to take a regular Ford F-150 or a Ford Super Duty to the next step on the off-road capability ladder. Effectively, it has the same goals as and competes directly against the Z71 package on the Chevy Silverado.

The FX4 package includes similar ingredients: specially-tuned off-road suspension, electronically locking rear differential (driver controlled), hill descent control, and three skid plates underneath to protect the front differential, transfer case, and the fuel tank. There are also several tire choices that can help take the F-150 or the Super Duty further up the trail.

Ford pickups that are configured with the FX4 package still come with the front air deflector, but the design is a little different from that of the Silverado. The air deflector is recessed further underneath the front of the truck. The result is a better approach angle. The F-150 has a slightly better clearance than the Silverado, and this also helps with the breakover and departure angles.

The F-150 FX4 is just ever so slightly ahead of the Silverado 1500 Z71 on the scale of off-road trucks. Both are very similarly configured, both have great powertrain options, and 4x4 systems with a low range transfer case. At the end of the day, and at your next off-road obstacle, the Ford has a narrow edge due to better clearance and approach/breakover/departure angles.

Ford Raptor

This being the summer of 2016, we are still between Ford Raptors. The first generation Ford SVT Raptor has been out of production since the 2014 model year, and the all-new second generation Raptor is still several months away (coming at the end of 2016).

Still, the Ford Raptor is the Ferrari of factory off-road pickup trucks. What does it mean? It has the stance, the hardware, and the capability to back up the looks.

It is designed specifically to take off-road abuse. The upcoming 2017 Raptor has a reinforced frame, unique suspension geometry, a wider track to accommodate more wheel travel and axle articulation, FOX Racing off-road shocks (three inches in diameter in the 2017 truck), and specifically designed BFGoodrich All-Terrain

T/A KO2 tires. These tires are among the best in the industry. The Raptor's rims are truly beadlock capable. It means you can bolt on an off-road only beadlock ring and air down the tires for increased traction, a smoother ride, or better floatation over sand. Naturally, the Raptor has a locking rear differential, a low range transfer case, and a TORSEN front differential which can automatically lock the front differential. The truck also has the next generation of Ford's terrain management system, which offers six distinct driving modes that help tackle various terrains.

The Raptor's strength is high speed desert running, and it is a purpose-built truck. It's not a package that enhances the regular truck's off-road capability, but it's a truck that deserves its unique name and the cool factor that comes with it. Neither the 2014 nor the 2017 were eligible or available for our 2016 Off-Road Truck of the Year testing. It will contend for the 2017 title next year, and it has a good chance at taking the prize.

Nissan Frontier PRO-4X

	Ground Clearance	Approach Angle	Breakover Angle	Departure Angle
Nissan Frontier Crew Cab 4x4	8.9 in	32.6 deg	20.5 deg	23.3 deg

The PRO-4X off-road package does for the Nissan Frontier what Z71 does for the Chevy Colorado and the All-Terrain does for the GMC Canyon. It sprinkles the extra off-road flavor on the already tough and capable midsize truck. Naturally, this includes the off-road tuned suspension, the driver-controlled locking rear differential, the hill descent control, and the off-road worthy tires.

The formula for off-road success is the same as that of the competition, but the Frontier leads the GM midsize truck twins in ground clearance and approach/breakover/departure angles. The Frontier PRO-4X is an honest midsize truck that does not try to be fancy. It can comfortably tackle difficult terrain alongside competitors from GM and Toyota. Perhaps only the Toyota Tacoma TRD Pro can go further.

Nissan Titan XD PRO-4X

	Ground Clearance	Approach Angle	Breakover Angle	Departure Angle
Nissan Titan XD Crew Cab 4x4	8.9 in	21 deg	20.2 deg	24.5 deg

The PRO-4X version of the new Titan XD is a solid off-road package. It includes the mandatory off-road tuned suspension, and the locking rear differential. We tested the PRO-4X on a very snowy and icy Gold Mine Hill. The truck had the hardware for the job. PRO-4X does not include running boards, which is a plus for off-roading as it improves the clearance and the breakover angle. Although, the Titan XD is a tall truck, so you need to give yourself a little boost to get into the cab. The General Grabber tires did well when we pulled up to the trailhead. We always stop on the steep part of the trail in order to make it more difficult for all trucks and to also make it fair to all. Not many trucks would have gone up that trail on that day. The packed layer of snow was hiding sheets of solid ice. The Titan XD dug in through the relatively grippy snow and onto the ice it went. There was not overcoming that place with a winch or tire chains.

Ram HD Off-Road

	Ground Clearance	Approach Angle	Breakover Angle	Departure Angle
Ram HD Crew Cab 4x4	7.1 in	21.8 deg	18.2 deg	22.3 deg

Ram has offered off-road worthy components on its heavy-duty trucks for a long time, but the Off-Road package for the 2017 Ram HD pickup bundles it all together, adds hill descent control and Bilstein monotube shocks, and puts a pretty bow on top. This package is aimed as a direct competitor to the Chevrolet Z71 and Ford FX4 heavy-duty trucks. This Ram HD package offers a limited slip differential instead of a driver-controlled rear locking differential.

We have not had a chance to wring this truck out on the off-road trails of the Rocky Mountains yet. However, I had a chance at a brief on-road drive in one of these. The Ram HD Off-Road package has an improved on-road ride quality, but the overall on-road comfort still does not beat the Ram Power Wagon or the Chevy HD with the Z71 package.

Ram Rebel

	Ground Clearance	Approach Angle	Breakover Angle	Departure Angle
Ram Rebel Crew Cab 4x4	10.3 in	25.4 deg	19.6 deg	23.0 deg

The Ram Rebel is the off-road leader of the Ram half-ton truck line-up. It was introduced as a 2015 model. It offers off-road prowess and the flair that goes along with it. The Ram 1500 Outdoorsman package was discontinued with the 2017 model year, so the Rebel is now the head of the spear for the Ram 1500 off-road trucks.

The Ram Rebel is equipped with Bilstein mono-tube shock absorbers, but they are part of an air suspension system that comes standard on all Rebels. This is the only truck on this list that rides on air. It offers a very comfortable ride on the highway when the suspension automatically switches into a lower highway setting. The truck offers an additional inch of suspension height over air suspensions in other ligh-duty Rams. When the truck is in its highest off-road suspension setting, the ride stiffens up significantly. Naturally, the Rebel offers underbody protection and an anti-spin differential for when the going gets tough. Toyo Open Country T/A tires complete the package.

The Rebel is a competent off-roader. I had a rare chance to drive a Rebel and a Power Wagon on a tough trail called the Backway to Crown King, Arizona. The Rebel did not do all the hardest sections of the trail, but it made it to the destination without getting stuck and with just barely a scrape on the front skid plate. If you put the Rebel's transfer case into 4-Low and pick your line, this is a truck that will take you to a remote location.

Toyota Tacoma TRD Pro

	Ground Clearance	Approach Angle	Breakover Angle	Departure Angle
Toyota Tacoma Crew Cab 4x4*	9.4 in	32 deg	21 deg	23.5 deg

* the numbers listed here are for the 2016 Tacoma TRD Off-Road package (not TRD Pro)

The Tacoma TRD Pro was first introduced for the 2015 model year. Since the truck was completely redesigned for 2016, the TRD Pro package went away while the company was launching all the other configurations and trim packages. The TRD Pro makes a return with the 2017 Tacoma.

The Tacoma with the TRD Off-Road package is already an off-road focused and capable rig. The TRD Pro takes the successful Tacoma 4x4 formula and turns it into the ultimate factory-prepared off-road Tacoma. Suspension is modified with 2.5-inch FOX off-road shocks and tuned front coilovers and rear springs. There is an additional one inch of ground clearance in the front and remote reservoirs for the rear shocks to decrease the chances of overheated shocks after high speed off-road running. There is also a substantial quarter-inch thick aluminum skid plate in the front that protects the powertrain components.

The 2015 Tacoma TRD Pro was simply tough as nails. Nathan Adlen and I took one on a moderate Rocky Mountain trail and the truck did not even blink an eye or put a wheel wrong. While we have not yet tested the 2017 TRD Pro, it promises to bring the same level of toughness and even more capability with the latest crawl control and traction control systems.

Toyota Tundra TRD Pro

	Ground Clearance	Approach Angle	Breakover Angle	Departure Angle
Toyota Tundra Crew Cab 4x4*	10.6 in	26 deg	n/a	22 deg

The TRD Pro boosts the Toyota Tundra a few steps above where the already capable Tundra TRD Off-Road resides. It offers additional 0.2 inches of ground clearance and an additional degree of departure angle. Every little bit helps.

Toyota does not list the breakover angle for the truck, but warns that adding a Tow Package to the Tundra significantly affects the departure angle. The angle drops from 22 degrees to 16 degrees, which is a significant decrease.

2016 Gold Hitch Off-Road Truck of the Year: Ram Power Wagon

	Ground Clearance	Approach Angle	Breakover Angle	Departure Angle
Ram Power Wagon Crew Cab 4x4	14.3 in	33.6 deg	23.5 deg	26.2 deg

Finally, here it is! The 2016 Off-Road truck of the year. Just like the Ford Raptor is a purpose-built off-road truck in the half-ton truck class, the Ram Power Wagon is the off-road bad boy among the heavy-duties. The name and original design were born from the military trucks of World War II. The truck was converted to civilian use after the war and the rest is history. The Power Wagon name went away for more than two decades, but then was resurrected in 2005 as an off-road version of the Dodge Ram 2500. It is now simply referred to as the Ram Power Wagon.

The Ram Power Wagon rides on beefy axles with low 4.10:1 differential gear ratios. The front and rear axles have driver-controlled locking differentials. No other factory-prepared pickup truck offers selectable locking diffs front and rear. The ride is dampened with the help of Bilstein mono-tube shock absorbers. An electronically disconnecting front sway bar provides even more front axle articulation. This truck comes with a winch from the factory. Ample ground clearance, good approach/breakover/departure angles, and Goodyear Duratrac tires round out the package.

The Power Wagon comes in a crew cab configuration, but it still has the best breakover angle of this bunch. This truck is simply an off-road beast. It tackled steep rocky sections of the Backway to Crown King trail, which looked impossible for any vehicle this size. Driving this truck off-road instills ultimate confidence. The driver still needs to be aware of the trail they are on, but the Power Wagon commands the earth into submission and gets you over the obstacles. On the way to Crown King, the Power Wagon never scraped on any rock or put a wheel wrong. We never had to use the winch.

The truck made easy work of our Gold Mine Hill test trail, ignoring the fact that it was covered in packed snow and ice. There was no argument that this truck should be the winner of the 2016 off-road truck award.

The Power Wagon gets a refresh for the 2017 model year. This includes a new grille, graphics, colors, and a more upscale interior. It only gets better from here.

MR. TRUCK & ANDRE

15

THE FUTURE OF PICKUP TRUCKS

THE PAST REPEATS ITSELF

THE NEXT GENERATION

You've heard nothing is new and history repeats itself. There is hope in that; my bell bottoms from the seventies should be coming back anytime now. Trucks are like that. In the seventies, our cars were boats, quality was poor, and fuel mileage was ridiculous. Japanese cars had invaded the Continent and Detroit was scrambling to save market share. We were in an oil crisis and lines at the gas station had us worried. I remember when the 500-cubic-inch Cadillac showed up. It only lasted one year.

Our big V-8s gave way to turbocharged 4-cylinders. Ford reacted with the Mustang SVO and Thunderbird turbos. It was probably those old geezers at Ford who remembered the seventies and decided the future truck engine had to be a V6 twin turbo gasser.

Now we're up to Generation 2 of the 3.5L Ecoboost that produces the most torque (470 pound-foot at 3,500 RPM) in the half-ton segment. This EcoBoost is backed up by a 10-speed automatic tranny. I grew up thinking a 4-speed auto with overdrive like I have in my 1970 Chevy C10 was the cat's meow.

Engine downsizing and turbocharging are here again.

It's 2016, and the GM midsize Colorado and Canyon have the famous Thailand "baby Duramax" diesel that gets 30 MPG on the highway. These 4-bangers have an exhaust brake and integrated trailer brake controller. But these aren't the first diesels in midsize — or minis as we called them — in the eighties, everyone had a little diesel: Ford Ranger, Chevy S10, Chevy LUV from Isuzu, Nissan truck, Toyota truck, and Mitsubishi. Turbos weren't involved yet, but the little oil burners were heavy-duty, with cylinder sleeves and mechanical injector pumps, and got decent fuel mileage.

Big news in 2016 was the Nissan Titan XD with a Cummins turbo-diesel. It's the in-between truck: not a half-ton, and not a three-quarter ton. Being a diesel in-between is news. But Ford, Dodge and GM had an in-between truck in the early eighties that was half-ton with 8-bolt wheels and an extra leaf spring. It wasn't heavy-duty and didn't have a full-floating rear axle. It confused buyers like the Titan XD does. On GM, you could tell the heavy-duty from the poser ligh-duty, because the heavy-duty had plastic fender flares.

Ford did it again in 1997 with a 7-bolt F250. Again, it was a half-ton with different wheels, a slightly heavier suspension, but no full-floating axle. And the odd 7-bolt wheels were expensive. I hope Ford doesn't relive the holey frames from 1980-1982. To save weight and hopefully improve fuel mileage, Ford put holes all over their truck frames. Later in 1982, they came out with a kit to plug the holes. They were only in heavy duties the first year, but stayed in the light-duties for three years.

In some cold, salted-highway states, the salt would rot out the rear frame, or worse, behind the rear bumper, with holes and crack. I've seen rear bumpers facing straight down. Wonder what happened to the trailer? I hope the holey frames don't come back, but there will be lighter truck frames coming.

What Happens Next?

The following areas of pickup truck development will be hotly contested over the next decade: diesel, hybrid and electric powertrains, usage of advanced lightweight materials such as carbon fiber or Barotex, and autonomous driving.

CAFE standards are getting tougher. Large light truck EPA combined economy averages for the fleet stay at 19 MPG until 2021, but then sharply grow to 23 MPG by 2025. Basically, all trucks sold in a given year by a manufacturer must meet these efficiency goals after you average all of them out. Failure to do so will result in penalties.

Powertrains

Undercarriage of a traditional gasoline V8 pickup truck

Many companies are already working on turbo-diesel, hybrid, plug-in hybrid, or electric trucks to satisfy tougher efficiency standards. Ram did well with the introduction of a light-duty 3.0L V6 EcoDiesel engine in the Ram 1500. It continues to be very popular, and it shows consumer appetite for more efficient powertrains in mainstream pickups. Ford is rumored to be testing a turbo-diesel engine for the 2018 Ford F-150. All we have to go on for now are several spy photos of camouflaged test trucks.

There is another intriguing development at Ford. On December 14, 2015, company CEO, Mark Fields, made two important announcements on an NPR interview with Ari Shapiro. The piece of news that truck buyers and enthusiasts should be interested in has to do with hybrid F-Series trucks: Mark said that the company is preparing a rear-wheel drive hybrid [F-Series] truck before the end of the decade (2020).

Ford is not alone in looking at electrification of pickup trucks. GM is again producing and selling a limited number (700 in total) of mild-hybrid light-duty Chevy Silverado and GMC Sierra pickup trucks. This system is called "eAssist." It combines an electric motor that is rated at 13 HP and 44 pound-foot of torque with the 5.3L V8 to allow the gas-burner to spend more time enjoying V4 cylinder deactivation mode. Chevrolet claims eAssist electric hybrid will boost fuel economy by 13 percent for an EPA rating of 18/24/20 MPG city/highway/combined. These trucks are currently only available for California customers. The eAssist option adds a reasonable $500 to the price of the trucks.

There are other smaller companies, such as VIA Motors, who convert GM trucks and commercial vans into plug-in gas-electric hybrids. A Chevy Silverado 1500 that has been converted into a VIA Motors VTRUX can go about 40 miles on electricity alone, and has a 4.3L V6 gasoline engine/generator to replenish the batteries for a total range of 400 miles. VTRUX's payload of 1,000 pounds is not very high, but it demonstrates that a plug-in hybrid pickup truck is already possible and viable for some businesses.

Ram is working to redesign its light-duty and heavy-duty trucks. You can be sure that they are looking at new ways to boost efficiency. It may be the next generation of the 3.0L EcoDiesel V6 or a gas-electric hybrid system that is similar to the one in the 2017 Chrysler Pacifica minivan. Nissan is working on a new V6 gasoline engine for the next generation light-duty Titan. And Toyota is surely not standing by to let everybody else overtake them with the latest powertrains.

Lightweight Materials

Everybody must know by now that Ford introduced an aluminum bodied F-150 for the 2015 model year. Yes, there was one day when many Ford executives got together and decided to shift construction of the most popular vehicle in the country (the F-150) from a steel body to aluminum. This was a ballsy move, but it's starting to pay off after some serious heavy lifting and many years of hard work. Many luxury cars are also constructed out of aluminum, and some, like the BMW 7-series, are switching to carbon fiber-intensive body structures. While others, like the Cadillac CT6, found ways of combining many different lightweight materials to build a car.

Why couldn't pickup trucks follow the same formula? Why can't a pickup truck be made out of carbon fiber, at least partially? It does not have to be carbon fiber: there is also a new type of fiber called Barotex (http://www.barotex.com). This type of material promises great things, but it's not fully commercialized yet. Barotex is claimed to be environmentally-friendly, recyclable, light-weight, strong, water and fire resistant, and it's based on volcanic rock for its base material. It's not a petroleum-based product. It sounds like the work of science fiction, but there are teams working hard to bring this strong and lightweight material into many industries, including automotive.

Barotex Technology Corporation claims: "Barotex can be used to create everything from the chassis, suspension, body, interior, and even the engine block of a car. Since Barotex is so strong and light-weight, it can increase vehicle performance, safety and mileage." This is a tall promise, but one that will be interesting to follow. You could argue that if a truck is made too light, then it will not be as stable when towing a heavy trailer. Yes, it may be the case, but other technologies, such as electronic truck and trailer sway control among others, will help trucks get lighter, more efficient, and quicker.

Autonomous Driving

2016 Ford F-150: adaptive cruise control and lane keep assist systems

Driver-aid technologies are proliferating across the automotive world. Many luxury cars are now approaching full autonomy. Technology is not quite there as of 2016, but it's getting very close. There are technologies such as adaptive cruise control that keep a distance between you and the vehicle ahead, active lane keep assist that helps you stay in your highway lane by steering, blind spot monitoring, a self-park system, and more.

Naturally, this spurs controversy and concern about safety. Can we really trust our cars and trucks to drive themselves? One hundred percent vehicle autonomy is still many years, if not decades, away, but it's not to say that trucks cannot negotiate multilane highways autonomously in a couple of years. Ford has already entered this world with adaptive cruise control and lane keep assist systems. GM is not far behind with a collision warning system. This technology already exists in their cars, so it's just a matter of time for it to proliferate into pickups. This is another way that will take us ever closer to the $100,000 pickup truck.

MR. TRUCK

16

OIL CHANGE MYTHS
BONUS ROUND
TAILGATE MYTH

WHEN TO CHANGE YOUR OIL?

We keep hearing about changing oil every 3,000 miles. Then why does your new truck owner's manual say 15,000 miles between oil changes? The point that keeps us confused is that the oil viscosity keeps getting more like water in new trucks. I grew up with 10W40 and thicker. To get better fuel mileage with less friction in engines, transmission, and axles, truck manufacturers use lighter viscosity oil, allowing all the moving parts to move easier. Some are 5W20. The new 2017 Ford F-150 EcoBoost has a 10-speed automatic transmission that has "ultra low viscosity" oil to make it all work, including the automatic shutting off of the engine when you idle. Ultra low viscosity sounds more like water than an oil pour rate.

With lighter oil, does that mean less protection and more wear? And if the oil change interval is longer, will dirtier oil cause more wear? I can see why informed folks worry about going more miles between fresh oil and new oil filters. I worry when service centers are preaching 3,000-mile oil changes no matter what. When truck manufacturers put their warranty and reputation behind the longer oil change interval, it makes you believe their recommendation.

Synthetic oil is man-made, not the same thing that *Beverly Hillbillies*' Jed Clampett found when he shot the dirt and "Up through the ground came a-bubblin' crude, Oil that is, Black Gold, Texas Tea." (I miss Elly May, but that's another story.) Crude oil has differently sized molecules. Synthetic oil is like a designer oil, made better in the lab with the same size molecules. This makes the oil degrade less, lubricate better, and last longer. Invented for the Sabre Jet engines used in the Korean war, synthetic oil has been around for decades. Top brands are Amsoil, Mobil One, and Royal Purple.

The new super oils available today help truck manufacturers improve fuel consumption, lubricate better, and pass the new crazy emissions laws. This all comes to play when Ram, with Cummins diesel, can recommend 15,000-mile oil change intervals. In your truck's owner manual under service schedules, a chart will show you a severe schedule (for towing trailers and dusty work) and a normal schedule.

When I drove a bulldozer for a living, the county would do oil analysis to see how much brass, copper, and other minerals were in the oil. That told the techs what was wearing in the engine and when to change oil. The military has a similar analysis system for a service schedule. GM started using algorithms onboard that would measure how long the engine idled, how long the engine ran at higher RPMs, etc. This was to allow an onboard computer to measure if you were towing a trailer or idling a lot to decide how often to change your oil. The message would come on in the truck's dash and tell you to "change oil soon." Now several truck and car manufacturers use a similar system.

So do you listen to your truck or the oil change companies that probably make more money if you change your oil more often? Truck manufacturers have more risk on the line if they are wrong when the truck tells you to change your oil, or even if your truck's manual tells you to change oil at 15,000 miles. Without synthetic oil, GM Oil Life Monitor System will give you the "change oil" warning from 7,000 miles to 12,000 miles (except for certain performance Chevy cars). You have to reset the automatic monitoring systems after you change your oil.

These are the facts. You decide who to believe. Oil is the work force for long engine life. Many semi-trucks have an oil interval of 15,000 to 25,000 miles for severe duty. But they hold 40 quarts of oil, so they can dilute more dirt. Oil viscosity on a typical semi-truck diesel is 10W40 with more going to 5W40.

My truck is telling me this week to change the oil. Who are you going to call? OIL MYTH BUSTERS.

Tailgate Myth

Tailgate up or down for better fuel mileage? Redneck logic would say tailgate down will have less air resistance. But there is turbulence behind the cab that goes in strange directions. When the rear sliding windows first came out, we all tried them. But if you had hay or dirt in the truck bed, it would suck it into the cab. The folks with money used wind tunnels to solve the mystery. What they discovered was with the tailgate up, the air coming over the cab into the bed formed an air bubble in the bed. This allowed air to flow over the bed and across the top of the tailgate. If you want to prove this yourself, tape some streamers on the rear edge of the top of your truck cab. Then put streamers on top of the tailgate. You could also put streamers at the bottom of the truck's rear glass. Then have someone drive the truck while you drive next to your truck. Now you have your own wind tunnel without spending millions. Or just drive the truck with tailgate up and down and record your fuel mileage.

Tailgate up or down?

NATHAN ADLEN

BONUS CHAPTER

REVIEWING TRUCKS, IT'S HARDER THAN IT LOOKS

ROADTRIP MISADVENTURE

In the spring of 2003, my editor said, "Go out and do an adventure review." That was it. There was no reference to a location, theme, or even a vehicle. I was on my own. I simply needed to make something creative rather than something technical. Awesome, no problem, it's got to involve a truck – easy!

Looking up and regurgitating numbers can be tedious. Technical bits take time and a great deal of methodical fact-checking. Driving a car around for a week is enjoyable, but when the entire experience has to be summed up in a few hundred words intertwined with numerous technical details, it can feel like data entry over creative expression.

Driving a truck around could be something different, right? While I had occasional exposure to trucks, I never evaluated one other than writing up basic information. These were numbers printed on a page, no real-world experience, it was the basics for folks who only needed the basic information. Or so I thought.

My model for that publication was: facts, facts, experience, facts, and conclusion – in 1,100 to 1,300 words. My experience with these reviews gave me great confidence for the upcoming adventure. I had great admiration for the automotive writers who hit the open road, bounced around off-road, and forged new trails while reviewing their vehicle. Logic dictated: read up on their technique and make it my own.

After a few days of doing research, watching the *Indiana Jones* trilogy, finding cool off-road videos, and asking around about a truck, the whole trip was planned. I would take a truck towing a trailer to Moab, Utah. I was considering driving an easy trail like Gemini Bridges or another scenic trail that would look good on camera (this was the early days of digital cameras where a massive, expensive DSLR was the only way to shoot stills) and allow me to return the truck unscathed. While there, I would camp, off-road, hike, and ride. A great way to dip my toe into the water of real adventure journalism.

I got my hands on a 2004 Ford Ranger with the new FX4 Level II off-road package. It was perfect. Equipped with a powerful 4.0-liter SOHC V6 that cranked out 207 horsepower at 5,250 RPM and 238 pound-foot of torque at 3,000 RPM, it came with an updated five-speed manual transmission that was as easy to use as a manual from a passenger car. It had beefy BF Goodrich All-Terrain T/A Tires, Alcoa forged aluminum wheels, Bilstein shocks, and a Torsen limited-slip differential. It was just right for an off-road adventure, and it could tow up to 5,560 pounds!

Rather than acquire this truck from Ford directly (thus insuring it was in top condition and backed by the automaker), I "borrowed" one from a friendly dealership. This is how I got many of my vehicles for reviews back then. In exchange, I would write ads or copy for the dealership. Usually, the vehicle's past was never brought up, as I never had any issues. When I noticed the 10,000-plus miles on the odometer, I ignored it.

Failing to find a suitable trailer from any friends or dealers, I rented a 6x12, dual axle, white-and-rust colored cargo trailer that weighed 1,990 pounds empty. Several adventure guys used rented trailers to haul and sleep in. Hell, I would be able to include a towing review in my piece, too! I loaded it with a 400 pound quad bike, a 600 pound John Deere Gator, (full) fuel containers, camping supplies for two, and two bikes.

I thought the trailer probably weighed just under 4,000 pounds loaded, but experience has taught me that a load and trailer like this was well over 5,000 pounds. No problem, that's way under the maximum rating, I thought.

Ballast, unused electric brakes, no brake controller, maximum towing for a 2004 Ford Ranger 4x4 with a manual transmission, funny noises, bad smells, and utter failure were all factors I was about to learn. This is where modern-day, properly schooled and prepared truck reviewers have the upper hand. They have the factors fully calculated before they embark on any type of review. Here are the facts that professional truck reviewers would have calculated before departing:

Vehicle's condition: It turns out that the 2004 Ford Ranger 4x4 FX4 Level II was a lease return. It had transmission and electrical issues. These issues had yet to be addressed.

Maximum towing: A 2004 Ford Ranger with 4X4 and a manual transmission can tow 3,100 pounds, not 5,000-plus. Never mind the flagrant overloading of the tongue-weight (300 pounds max vs over 400 pounds) or the overall GVWR. After revisiting the weights and doing further research, the GVWR was exceeded by (at least) 1,000 pounds.

Trailer's condition: This trailer came from a local, less-reputable purveyor of rental trailers. Mentioning that the rear axle made a funny noise would have been helpful. At the very least, a professional would have made sure that the wheel bearings were greased... three were.

Weight distributing hitch: Most of these types of hitches ensure a level ride. It corrects the tow vehicle's rear-end sag, improves overall ride, and, when properly equipped, corrects trailer sway. Without a weight distributing hitch, your rear sags, nose lits, front-end lightens, suspension architecture becomes overloaded, and your trailer wanders.

Trailer brakes: No automotive journalist with an ounce of logic would drive a trailer this heavy without brakes. While the Ford did come with a light hookup, there was no brake controller. That means that, on top of its own weight, the little Ford truck had to do the braking for a 4,000-plus-pound trailer. An aftermarket trailer brake controller could have been installed in around an hour and saved a lot of grief.

Safety equipment: Having chalks for the wheels, mirror extenders, a spare tire, proper jack, fire extinguisher, extra chains, rope, gloves, tools, and other essentials would have been smart. On every truck review that requires a trailer, these precautions are always taken into consideration.

A balanced load: Stacking a four-wheel piece of farm equipment with a quad-bike past the axles increased the tongue-weight. It also contributed to a very uneven ride. Placing more of the weight over the trailer's axle would have helped.

It's pretty obvious: the problems were mounting from the get-go. The whole point of doing the research and proper preparation is to ensure you have all of the bases covered before you begin to chronicle your story. When well-prepared automotive journalists, like The Fast Lane Truck team, take on an obstacle, they do it with full knowledge of the truck and the equipment that will be used with the truck.

There's more. Over the years, it has become apparent that the truck customer is (usually) immersed in as many facts and figures as they can obtain about their truck, far more in tune with every shred of information about their vehicle than the equivalent car consumer, wants the facts tested, and they know the numbers. Add passion and a sense of individual brand-name pride to the mix, and you have a truck connoisseur. Woe be unto the automotive journalist who forgets how passionate a truck connoisseur is.

I departed with my friend early on a Thursday morning with the trailer loaded, coolers packed, cigars in a travel humidor, and plenty of munchies for the road. Denver to Moab is 354 miles, and can be driven in about six hours by an average driver. Considering the extra load, I gave myself seven hours – no problem. If everything went well, we would return on Tuesday.

We'll call my passenger "Jack" because he lacked the ability to use one properly.

I noticed that the steering of the 2004 Ford Ranger felt a bit light. Looking into my rear-view mirror, I observed that I may have been at a slight angle. Never mind the four-or-more inches of squat after I hooked up the trailer, and never mind the medium-sized Ranger mirrors being unable to see past the trailer on either side. This load was heading for Moab!

Note: The 2004 Ford Ranger 4x4 FX4 Level II came with an outstanding Pioneer® Sound system, which included a 290-watt unit with an in-dash, six-disc MP3 player, and seven speakers.

I could tell the little Ford was struggling as we headed up Interstate 70, climbing to over 11,000 feet. I never got it out of third-gear once we began to ascend. I did feel the trailer sway a bit, too. "No big deal," I thought as I cranked up the Led Zeppelin on that Pioneer® Sound system, "we're making it to Moab in seven hours!"

The grinding noise of an axle bearing beginning to seize is noisy and unsettling, which I might have known if my eardrums weren't bleeding from British rock and Jack's poor singing. It would have alerted me to what was coming.

As the Ford Ranger slowed, nearly to dangerously reduced speeds, I came upon a fully-loaded tractor-trailer cruising at just about our speed. I pulled behind him, relaxed my acceleration a bit, and "drafted" the big boy as we headed towards the Eisenhower Tunnel and 11,155 feet above sea level. Easy as pie.

We were already near empty on fuel as we entered the tunnel. I figured I would coast down from the tunnel into Silverthorne, CO, which is 9,035 feet, over 2,000 feet down from where I was, and grab some gas. No problem.

Just as we began our decent, I noticed that at any speed over 50 MPH, the trailer shook and wagged so violently that we nearly knocked our heads together in the cab. I kept my foot on the brake and kept the truck in fourth-gear. This was no big deal.

By the time we pulled off in Silverthorne, we could smell over-heated brakes and the trailer swayed more noticeably than ever.

Focusing on the Ford Ranger's brakes (and being too stupid to bother inspecting the trailer's wheels) during the gas stop, I felt that, being that it took a while to fuel up, the brakes would be fine. I did have enough wherewithal to buy clip-on mirrors, which helped immensely. Surely, this forethought would mitigate future issues?

We traveled slowly, still experiencing a turbulent ride. We had an ace up our sleeve. By switching from British rock to the Beastie Boys, we would blast the tunes and still make Moab in around seven hours. It's amazing how much noise you can drown out when you're blasting music, singing your heads off, and driving a horse named "Paul Revere!" (*That's a reference to a Beastie Boys song, my redneck friends*).

As Interstate 70 heads west, it begins to narrow and it gets pretty curvy. You truly notice it if you're alongside a large truck and trying desperately to pass them as quickly as possible for fear of being crushed. Well, imagine passing a rusty trailer weaving unpredictably on the road like a flag in a gale. That's what many drivers contended with as they tried to scurry past.

We earned many middle-finger salutes.

Then all hell broke loose. As traffic was picking up speed after passing through a construction zone just east of Glenwood Springs, CO., we heard a "BANG!" followed by a shuttering that corresponded with the trailer shaking back-and-forth like a poorly trained bellydancer.

Immediately, the little Ford felt a jerk like someone threw an anchor into soft sand behind the trailer.

Cars began to honk and several windows unrolled to point to our rear trailer axle. Finally doing something almost intelligent, I pulled off on the first exit I could access. Music off, windows open, I could clearly hear a skidding noise that forced both of us to react like two chimpanzees screaming in fear. The air smelled of melting rubber and burning gear oil, and the sound of car horns filled our ears.

The trailer felt like it was getting heavier and heavier each foot we crawled down. I had to shift into second-gear and slam my foot down just to move the proceedings to the entrance of the CDOT public parking area for Hanging Lake and Colorado River. Finally, just as we entered the parking area, the truck simply stopped pulling. I could add the smell of burning clutch to my list of new smells.

"Must be a flat," I said stupidly.

The smoking evidence of our stupidity lay before us. It would be concluded later that the wheel from the driver's side front axle of the trailer came off and jammed itself under the rear axle (hence the smoke, burning rubber and heavy resistance in towing). It came off because the wheel-bearing froze and eventually helped shear off the hub.

One of the first things you learn when becoming a journalist is to answer who, what, when, where, and why. These questions are the very cornerstones of journalism, and every automotive journalist worth a damn knows how to answer these questions as effectively as possible. These basic questions can be used to create just about any type of news story.

Here's an example:

Who? Nathan and Jack, two idiots who knew nothing about prepping a truck and trailer for a trip. Two journalists who could have researched the basics of trailering and, perhaps, asked a few questions from experts. Sadly, they let laziness and ineptitude get in their way.

What? A 2004 Ford Ranger 4x4 FX4 Level II pickup truck and a trailer that was built before the Kennedy Administration. The truck suffered from a few known ailments that a simple inquiry could have answered. The trailer was rented via some guy with a dirt farm near Greeley, CO.

Where? Well, that's one of the fun questions. The story should have been centered in Moab, but the wagon train lost its "ho" not even half way there. In fact, it's just stupid luck that the two imbeciles made it to the CDOT public parking area. Anywhere else on that highway and we would have caused a major traffic jam, something Mr. John Law disapproves of.

When? That's another funny part. Early spring in the Rocky Mountain region tends to mean snow. In this case, we had some light snow leading up to the drive and, wouldn't you know it, heavy snow right where we broke down. That's not the worst of it. Getting back over the pass, through the tunnel, and back down into Denver when there's heavy snow is no picnic.

Why? This is the rub: I could have selected any number of paths and things would have gone better. Doing my due diligence on the truck and trailer would have been a good start. Truck journalists who have some experience would have (most likely) seen and fixed many of the obstacles I missed. Weighing the truck and trailer would have been a good idea to begin with.

Conclusion:

Bloody knuckles, bruised arms, and strained backs. Using a partially broken bumper jack, multi-tool, and an ill-fitting tire-iron finally freed the wayward wheel. Once I paid several hundred bucks to flatbed the trailer back to its extremely upset owner, we drove the Ford Ranger back to Denver. Several warning lights came on, and the truck's top engine speed could not exceed 2,500 RPM without the engine dying. What took three hours to reach took an additional eight hours to retreat from.

The trip was ruined, I spent three times what I would have made, my friend was pretty upset, the dealership was not pleased, and I felt like an idiot. I like to think that learning from a negative experience makes people wiser, and that was definitely the case here.

It's taken years of research, asking questions, and trial and error to discover that, even now, I still get it wrong. Reviewing trucks is a hard business. Thirteen years after my debacle, I'm still trying to get it right.

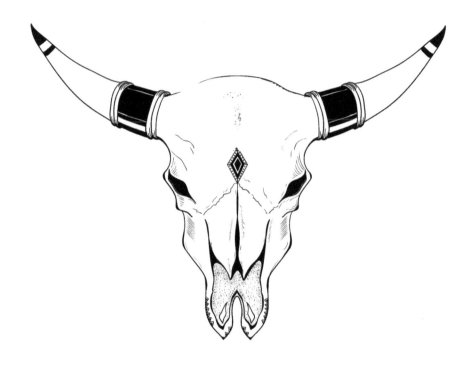

AUTHOR BIOS

H. Kent Sundling, (Mr. Truck), spent his first thirty years on the farm. In high school, Sundling sorted cattle after school for local farmers, ditch loading his Quarter Horse in the back of his pickup truck. Over a million miles towing large trailers and wearing out trucks on the farm led to his next career, selling trucks in Denver for ten years. Auto buyer for AAA Auto Club selling all brands and Internet truck sales at a dealership involved Mr.Truck in his first website in 1999. Ford Motor managers named Sundling "Mr. Truck" when they picked him as one of the top four truck salesman in the country. For Ford, Mr.Truck did live truck training on Ford-Star TV and some truck training videos.

Ten years later, on to automotive journalism, Mr.Truck built a couple dozen websites about towing trailers and started his truck and trailer review column in horse and farm magazines. As part of the national press, Mr.Truck gets invited to new truck media launches and horse trailer factories for review. Visit www.MrTruck.com, reviews of trucks, SUV's, trailers and accessories and install articles.

Andre Smirnov is a life-long automotive enthusiast. He emigrated from Russia to the United States in 1992 and moved directly to Colorado. He worked at a mechanic's shop while in high school and went to the University of Colorado, earning a degree in computer science and software engineering. He worked in the computer industry for nearly fifteen years and holds a U.S. patent on distributed data transfer. He began trucking and towing trailers as a regular consumer in the early 2000s and has worked at TFL since 2011. Andre became the managing editor of TFLtruck.com in 2013 and reviews and tests new trucks on a regular basis. He also travels around the country to truck manufacturer events, auto shows, auctions, and more. Andre's American Dream is in full swing and it's still evolving. Trucks are his life, and what a great life it is!

CPSIA information can be obtained
at www.ICGtesting.com
Printed in the USA
BVHW092044111019
560875BV00002B/2/P